THE LIGHTWORKER'S GUIDE
TO HEALING GRIEF

THE LIGHTWORKER'S GUIDE TO HEALING GRIEF

Tina Erwin

ARE PRESS

ASSOCIATION FOR RESEARCH AND ENLIGHTENMENT

A.R.E. Press • Virginia Beach • Virginia

DISCLAIMER

The contents of this publication are intended for educational and informative use only. They are not to be considered directive nor as a guide to self-diagnosis or self-treatment. Before embarking on any therapeutic regimen, it is absolutely essential that you consult with and obtain the approval of your personal physician or health care provider.

Cover design by Christine Fulcher

Dedication

This book is dedicated to the life and memory of Arianna Rose, "Cutie Pie," Harris. Although you left us physically at the tender age of six, you live in our hearts forever.

This book is also dedicated to Arianna's mother, and my wonderful sister, Andrea Debs Harris, her patient and kind husband, Craig, and their courageous daughter, Marisa.

Finally, this book is dedicated to all those who are left behind, who are in the learning phase of acceptance of the transition of a loved one or who have experienced any type of grief.

Contents

Acknowledgments

I would like to gratefully acknowledge the critical input of my sister Andrea Harris, her husband, Craig, and my niece, Marisa.

I also appreciate the love and support of my husband, Troy, and my children and their spouses: James and Amee, Andrew and Monica, and to Jeanne Marie and her boyfriend, Michael.

I deeply appreciate the contributions of my brothers Paul and Pierre and all of our friends and extended family.

I send my most profound gratitude to my teacher, Tashi.

I want to give special thanks to my dear friends who took the time to read and help edit this work: Barbara, Vicki, Gwyn, Diane, Jackie, Robert, Stephanie, Tammy, Caryn, Nancy, and Karen.

I am deeply grateful to my daughter, Jeanne Marie, to my daughter-in-law, Monica, and to my sister, Andrea, for their long hours of editorial work on this book. Thanks, ladies, you did a great job!

FOREWORD

It is exquisitely painful, mind–boggling, mind–numbing, unfathomable, and unrealistic all at the same time. How can this be?
How can this be that my smart, beautiful, healthy, giggling, baby-
doll–playing little six–year–old girl is now dead? How can she be
talking to me one minute and then gone, dead, the next? How
does this happen? This is not in the natural order of things—children are not supposed to die before their parents, but mine did. A
child full of life and potential does not just die, but mine did. This
happens to other parents, not us, right? Wrong. As my husband,
my daughter, and I tried to come to terms with the grief, the realization, the reality, and the finality of the loss of our daughter, we
are grateful that we had help, and, boy, did we need it.

The quiet, sudden death of our daughter instantly threw my
family into a tailspin, taking us down a seemingly dark hole of
hopelessness, sadness, and grief. We felt sick with sadness. We felt
sick to our stomachs with grief and with the tremendous rush of
adrenalin caused by the sudden loss of our beloved and treasured
daughter.

The help that we received came immediately from our neighbors, emergency medical personnel, police, family, friends, classmates, teachers, school administrative staff, co–workers, and even
strangers. They provided emotional support, shoulders to cry on,
food, and guidance. However, I became immediately aware that

all these caring people were in just as much shock as we were. I think that people forget that individuals other than family members have special attachments to the one who died. They are also in a state of disbelief and sometimes fear, too. We all needed additional help and fast. The help came in the form of a 5'1" lady, short in stature but long on knowledge, experience and strength of character, determination and will—my sister, Tina.

I was in Virginia and she was in California, and yet she was able to be by my family's side within twenty–four hours! I sometimes wonder what that seven–hour plane trip must have been like for her. Tina was in just as much shock as we all were. How did she keep her composure, knowing that walking through our front door would be unlike any other visit? She was not coming for pleasure but to help us with the death of her beloved niece. All I can say is that she knew that she had a tremendous job to do. I believe that she put her feelings on hold to guide our family through the difficult times ahead. She even helped our friends and neighbors. Her presence here provided far more solace than she will ever know.

But who, you may ask, helped her? Did she grieve like the rest of us? Did she cry and scream into her pillow at night, just as we did? Was her pain just as exquisite as ours? Yes, most definitely. But she was armed with the power of spiritual insight. This spiritual awareness would en-able her to help all of us in time—and time is the key—to move forward into the future. She taught us how to move forward into a future with-out our daughter and yet a future not forever clouded by the heaviness of the shadow of grief. What was this knowledge? This knowledge is the spiritual understanding of the mechanics, physics, and science of death. Where did my child go? What happens on the other side? Will there be someone loving to meet her? Will we ever see her again? Tina had already had experience as a spiritual intuitive, and she used all of her knowledge to help us. There is nothing like experiencing something for yourself to broaden your knowledge. Everything that she had learned from twenty years of being a Naval Officer and from a lifetime of study-ing metaphysics was put into action.

It is my sincerest hope that the information in this book may be of assistance to those who are grieving and those who assist the grieving, whether it be family, friends, co-workers, hospice caregivers, or medical and emergency personnel. All souls return to their true home, the heaven world. My family and I will never stop for one moment missing our daughter, Arianna. However, now we have a better understanding of death, knowing where Arianna is and that we will see each other again in the heaven world.

Craig, Marisa, and I most sincerely thank our family members, Pierre, Paul and Linda, Cam and Anne, Stephanie, Elizabeth, and Marie who helped us with their prayers, love, and strength. We are sending a special thanks to Grandpa Don, who gave Arianna her first big hug in heaven. We are grateful to all of those courageous people who helped us during those turbulent times. Tina, we thank you for your wisdom, intelligence, strength, and courage during those times, now and into the future.

Andrea Harris

INTRODUCTION

Death comes to call on all of us, sometimes suddenly, sometimes after a long illness. However, for my family, death paid an extremely sudden call on March 14, 2003. On that fateful day, my six-year-old niece, Arianna Rose, died. She appeared to have had a mild cold and had missed a few days of school. She was usually incredibly healthy.

The afternoon she died, she had gone with her mom to pick up her older sister, Marisa, from school. Arianna seemed to be doing extremely well, recovering from her brief illness. They stopped and got a treat from a snack bar. They came home. Marisa and Arianna did homework, played on the computer, and said hello to friends across the way. She was in great spirits.

About 5:15 p.m., sitting next to her mom on the couch, Arianna told her mom she felt a little hot. Then she died. The rest is a blur that no parent ever wants to face, but many, many people do face.

How and why did this child die? The medical cause was Group A Strep, which we learned was extremely hard to diagnose and can strike very suddenly. The why has taken us longer, and, in fact, it is the *why* of her death that has lead to this book. It is a labor of love, for in the process of grieving this adorable child, we learned just how many other parents are grieving. We learned that, in truth, everyone is grieving someone or something. Consequently, this book is not just for us but also for anyone who is grieving anything. It is our sincerest hope that perhaps something in this book will be of service to you.

We also learned that no matter what happens to you or what job you have when someone dies, all of those who grieve need love and support for a very long time. This book is designed to help you who do the service of helping others to find the words, the deeds, and the hope that love never dies and that death is not the end. This book is for you, the Lightworkers, who are bringing the greatest good to everyone in these difficult situations.

Tina Erwin

How to Use This Tool Book

This is a spiritual tool book for any "lightworker" to have handy when death or disaster strikes. What is a lightworker? A lightworker is anyone who works for the greater good and seeks the wisest path to bring light to any situation.

This book is a reference guide as well as a guide to helping you find your compassionate heart to help yourself and others through the tough times. There are several ways to use this book:

• You can simply sit down and read it all the way through. This particular process will offer you a deeper insight into death, and you will learn what to do under a variety of circumstances.

• You may use it to look up whatever is your current concern, because each section will essentially stand alone. For instance, if you have to help an employee who has suffered the death of a child, or other family member, you can look up this specific section in Chapter 10 under "Employer Responsibilities."

• If someone close to you dies and you have to help a grieving family, you will want to understand how alone your friend or family member will be feeling, so chapters 2–5 and 9–12 will be especially helpful.

• If you have suffered the death of a child or spouse, you can read about those specific areas in chapters 2–5, 8, and 9–14.

• If you are being haunted by a ghost, read chapter 7.

• If you are dying yourself and you want to understand death, read chapters 1, 4, 5, 6, 7, 9, or basically the whole book.

- If your friend's pet dies, chapter 9 will be helpful.
- If you have to attend a funeral and you have no idea what to say, read this section in chapter 4: How to help a grieving person or family.

Whatever you do, be sure to read the jewel at the end of the book, the Quiet Profile in Courage. This section alone will help any reader appreciate that healing can take place no matter what has happened.

1

DEATH

Life *is* continuous, and is Infinite!
Edgar Cayce Reading 1554-2

What Is Death?

Every birth is a dawn and every death a night, one eternally folding into the other. Every night is alive with the light of the stars and the hope of the heavens, and every death is equally alive with the light of hope in the divine, the hope of life everlasting, and of rebirth.

Mortal people use the word *death* to define the end of mortal life. Many have come to believe that this word means the absolute end of all life. However, one of the goals of this book is to help you understand that the word *death* merely defines the boundary between one form of existence and another. The primary purpose of this book is to help anyone who is grieving anything to understand that all individuals can heal their grief over time.

There are as many forms of death as there are of grief. We know that there is physical death and death of creatures in our lives that we love. But there are other kinds of death that we grieve: death of a relationship, death through divorce, death through loss of job,

1

death through loss of physical or mental ability, death of innocence when uncovering past traumas, and death through the trauma of natural disasters, fires, floods, and the loss of possessions.

With the many forms of death that we encounter, the explanation of it could fill up many books. The simplest explanation, however, revolves around understanding energy. As children we learn that energy is neither created nor destroyed. If so, what happens when a person dies? Where does that energy go? Most of us never receive an answer, and, in fact, we are told that it is a different kind of energy and that the same laws do not apply. Yet the laws of physics do not change. So the quest begins to find out about the energy of life and of death, where it goes, and how it comes back again and again.

In this quest, we discover that energy has cycles. All objects have energy cycles, from washing machines to homes, from stones to water, and from people to animals. We can then say that we recycle the energy. Imagine a lake on the side of an Alpine mountain. In the warm summer heat, some of that water evaporates into the sky. It changes form and location. It becomes something entirely different. It becomes the clouds. As time progresses, the clouds become heavy, and the clouds release rain, or on a cold winter day, the water falls to the earth as snow and freezes on the top of the Alpine mountain. And yet again, the water has changed form and location. In the spring the ice melts, and it returns to the lake again. It is still water, and it still has the properties of water; it has not been created nor destroyed. But now it has been through several incarnations in several locations. It has gone on a journey, returning to where it began. The energy of life moves through existence like water, in cycles.

Using this analogy, we can begin to understand that death is merely a transition from one form and location to another. Transition means that we leave one form and move into another. The energy of a soul then takes on a different form. It sheds its physical body and enters a different state of existence where physical bodies are not required. It makes perfect sense. We celebrate the birth of people and animals as joyous, delightful, and full of promise, but if life and death are looked at as a cycle, then we should look upon death as simply returning to the place where our life force energy came from, the place where it is recharged, recycled, and recreated. We return home to the heaven world. However, to be able to return home, we all have to pass through the process of death. The process of death involves many people, especially the people who are grieving us. It, therefore, becomes important to understand all the concepts and types of death to enable us to embrace the concept of healing the grief that comes from the death of a person, a relationship, or a catastrophe.

Types of Death

There are many kinds of death and grieving. For some people, physical death does not end the relationship, since the love of another can last through eternity. For others, death is a cruel ending, but it doesn't have to be. We can choose how we will look at the absence of someone we love through any type of event, and there are numerous "absence events" in our lives.

From the painful separation of military deployments to the end of childhood as our children leave home for college or marriage, these seemingly "little deaths" make us grieve. There is the end of a relationship, as we have known it, through divorce, injury, and debilitating illness. Throughout our lives, we will encounter the constant changes that define life in a physical body. Often, these changes cause us to grieve or to "miss" that which we loved so much but now must change as we move forward with new challenges and experiences in our lives. Everything that has a beginning also has an ending. What that ending is, when it arrives, and how that ending comes will shape our response to each of these "ending" experiences. Each experience will determine our growth as a person and ultimately, our soul evolution.

So let us look at the various kinds of death so that we can understand people who are entering this dimension of transformation through grief and learn how to help them.

Physical Death

Physical death means that the person is just not coming through that front door anymore. You cannot hug, help, or comfort him or her, and the person who has died cannot comfort, help, or hug you. You cannot see the expression on the face and hear the laugh or the sound of his or her voice. There is a specific finality about death, a feeling of terrible permanence. This feeling can carry with it intense despair at the suddenness of a death or relief that the person, whom you have watched go through the torturous downward spiral to death, is finally at peace. Spiritual growth is sometimes stubbornly defined by how you approach and heal yourself at the death of someone you deeply love.

Mental Death

Mental death from brain damage, senile dementia, Alzheimer's, or mental illness creates a different kind of grief. The person you knew is simply not there, and the person who has replaced him or her is very different, needy, and unable to talk to you again in the way you are used to. This situation requires working through your grief as surely as any other aspect of a death. This is the death of a relationship. All that you knew is over, and, in some ways, it is truly as painful as physical death. With mental death, there is unending despair at the ever-increasing painful changes the person is going through. This is especially acute if the person does not remember who you are or were to him or her. There is also a sense of abandonment because that personality is never going to "be there" for you again although the body is physically there. In some ways, this is almost more painful than a physical death.

In this case, you must surely change course and stop the momentum of the old relationship. You must now chart the course for a new relationship, which is going to be challenging because this person's situation usually has a bleak prognosis. You must give yourself time to grieve. Everything has changed, and it won't ever be the same again. A parent becomes childlike. A child becomes mentally incapacitated, and while you want to feel as though the person is the same person, your loved one is not the same. Your roles have changed, and you are now a different person because of these changes.

You must grieve this situation just as surely as you would a physical death. Above all, you must be patient with yourself so that you can heal and adjust to this life change.

Accept that this is how life is going to be for the current future. Ask for help from friends and family or even certain agencies. Under no circumstances should you play the role of martyr. This performance serves only to destroy who you are. You have a huge job to do. Carrying out your work with grace will empower who you are. If you do it with martyrdom or bitterness, it will destroy you.

Take days off from the caregiving. Take a vacation. If necessary, take shifts with the care to feel like a normal person part of the time.

View the situation as happening for a reason or for the greater good, and find a friend or a really good spiritual practitioner or counselor to talk to about it. Do not take drugs or alcohol. These are depressants and are not helpful as you begin this uncharted journey. Be as clear thinking as possible. Insist on getting plenty of rest. Make rest a prime objective, for, without it, a cycle of depression can result, which will not serve anyone.

Abandonment

Many people feel that when death comes, there will be a sense of abandonment. This can be true. However, real abandonment occurs when a parent, spouse, or other family member walks out on a family. That person has not died but has decided not to be a part of that family anymore. It does not matter what the reason is; that person is not there. All people are going to respond to this differently, depending upon their position in the family, the age they are when the person left, and how the remaining family members handled it.

Each person in the family will have to grieve this significant loss. It can seem like a personal rejection of other family members. This may or may not be true. It is very easy to judge abandonment as being bad. Sometimes, it is very good for the person who leaves and better still for the family left behind. Some people are not meant to be together. Usually the process of someone leaving is fraught with emotion. Often, there is the added dynamic of loss of financial assistance. This can also create anger and bitterness.

The person who leaves will also have to grieve this event, knowing that he or she will be judged harshly. Often, things are just not what they seem.

It may take many years to understand why the event happened. If you conscientiously look for the reasons it happened and how it helped you to grow, you can use it as a positive tool in your soul evolution. If you allow it to create a bitter feeling in your heart, it will act like an acid, eating away at the foundation of your soul. Unrecognized, it can create a victim personality. The deciding aspect is in choosing which future you are ready to have—the one we know you deserve.

If you have had to live through an abandonment situation, you would be wise to look at the ways in which you have grown. This event will shape who you are and will help you to decide how you want your future to unfold. This type of grief can readily be healed through seeking the spiritual insight necessary to forgive all the parties and realize that you simply had a dynamic experience. You are still all right.

Divorce

Divorce is so common these days that it is the unusual child who has "original" parents still married to each other. No matter how many divorces there are, when it happens to a family, it usually causes a profound sadness, and all parties will grieve it in their own unique way. Yet it is even more than this.

Divorce is a shockwave that undermines any individual's concepts of love. For some, it is the end of family love—that unique nucleus of safety, security, and happiness. Divorce creates a sense of vulnerability that will always have to be grieved. The safe haven of your home no longer exists. The love you trusted and the people you trusted have betrayed you. Now you have to open an entirely new chapter of learning how to live and to love again when the love that was your foundation in life is shattered.

Frequently, divorce happens when teenagers are in high school. This tender time of changing hormones and emotional perceptions is challenging in an intact household. When divorce sits down at your kitchen table, often a rumbling rage is also its handmaiden. Frequently, the parents are so consumed with their own grief, guilt, and anger that they are of no immediate help to their bewildered and often depressed children. Seldom are there the financial resources to get immediate help for teenagers who may have been blindsided by their parent's actions. Parental behaviors span the range of sad on the modest end to powerfully violent at the extreme end. Children and teenagers find that a darkness enters their hearts and hope becomes hard to find.

A shredded heart takes a special kind of repair. For children, the grief can be especially poignant. They love both parents, but both parents do not love each other. Children cannot understand how a person can turn love on and off. Children feel divorce as an emotional betrayal on a profound level. To a child, a parent is like a god. This means that a parent is all-wise and all-knowing in the eyes of that young child. When a divorce comes, it is a spiritual betrayal of love to a child.

Children also become confused as to whether or not to love each parent equally. They may be afraid that the leaving parent has stopped loving them. Children may feel that the divorce is somehow their fault. They may be exceptionally confused about love. The aspect of either parent dating or being re-married will complicate this confusion. The loyalty issue will be ever constant in a child's mind.

To help children heal, allow them to talk about it. Allow them to ask any question they like. Patience during this time will become critical to the child's healing. Divorce is seldom convenient, and usually the emotions of all the parties are raw. People say things that echo in the ears of a child for a very, very long time. The healing of this situation will be challenging. The primary parent needs to be *available* to talk about what happened. Parents must also accept the responsibility for their part of the divorce. Telling the child what can be learned from this experience may be very healing. Do not say mean and cruel things about the other spouse, even if he or she is a really bad person. If it is at all possible, explain what happened. If either spouse made a really bad choice in choosing a mate, say that. Again, explain what has been learned. If the child likes the date or spouse of either parent, explain that you have an unlimited capacity to love and that loving another person for his or her good qualities does not diminish that child's love for either parent, nor does it define loyalty for either parent. Love is actually the only thing that will heal any divorce situation.

The sense of security all parties used to have is gone now. The couple made a commitment, and someone did not keep it. One of them becomes an alcoholic or abusive, and changes have to be made. This situation may seem like emotional abandonment. Another way to look at this is to realize that a different path has been chosen, one away from hurt. Grieving this choice will eventually move the family into a better place.

Sometimes you each have to realize that something has to end before something else can begin in your life. Grief is part of this process.

You can heal this pain by doing the grief work as well as working with a good grief counselor to learn how you can heal your life and your children's lives. You may also learn that healing your life will have been the reason for being in this situation in the first place.

Missing Persons

In the state of California alone, 25,000 persons are listed as missing. One day a loved one is here, and the next day that person is gone. For the vast majority of families, their loved one will never be found. Families must now be in contact with all kinds of law enforcement agencies. Some of these agencies will be kind and helpful, but for some people, the agencies will be difficult to handle. Families try to keep a case alive, but eventually, with few leads, families are left with the chilling fact that their loved one is just now a part of the ever-growing number of missing persons' files.

This is an especially cruel kind of grief: No body to bury, no information to say whether the person is dead or alive, and no one to ask. No answers. There are dead ends wherever you look. How do you grieve something that always carries with it one tiny bit of hope? Do you ever leave the house? What if the missing loved one decides to call or the authorities call? How do you function on a day-to-day level? If your child or family member were abducted, how would you deal with the looks and stares of friends or other family members endlessly wondering how this happened? Mostly you feel utterly frozen in time and space. You find yourself constantly looking in the faces of everyone who crosses your path, endlessly searching for your loved one. In essence, you become a very different person. It is as if who you were vanished that day, as well, and the person you have now become isn't someone you would have ever recognized.

One of the cruelest elements of this grief is the guilt. You replay the day it happened over and over a thousand times. You descend into the pit of "if only" and "what if" you had done this or that differently. What if you did or said something or noticed something or visited or stopped a situation or, or, or . . . You find yourself shying away from friends. You feel as though they are judging you. This is very hard. Truly, you are judging yourself for your own perceived failings. You just know you are somehow to blame. You will visit all the stages of grief. As the months and years go by, dullness sets in. The paradox of not knowing and yet endlessly hoping is a perpetual struggle in your slowly hardening heart.

There comes a day when you have to face the many fears attendant with this situation. Realizing that you attract what you fear the most, you must at some point decide to give up your fears and allow life to begin to flow again for you even though you do not have the person you love in your life.

You must reestablish your spiritual connection to God. You must ask for help in every step of this torturous process. You may not always understand why something happens, but you can trust that there will be a purpose for it at some point.

You can continue living. You can start by finding something to be genuinely happy about, even if it is for another person. If you can do this without guilt or feeling like you have betrayed the person who is missing, you will have begun to make significant progress.

There are things that you can do, however, that may help with living day-to-day. There does come a point when you must decide that you have to go on living. You can leave that part of your life on hold and still begin to function again. This aspect often takes a great deal of work in order to release the endless fear that the outcome of this missing person's case will be your worst nightmare.

Tell family and friends how to relate to the whole family. Leave things alone in the missing person's room for the first year. After that, create a new room. Start living again. Start finding things to be happy about. This is the hardest part: accepting the things that you can never change and understanding the things that are now forever changed.

Change in Life Situation—Physical Body

"Life is what happens to you while you are making other plans." This line from the movie *Mr. Holland's Opus* is what happens to you while you think you are going about your days, and then all of a sudden, something happens that changes everything. It can be a critical injury, an accident, a stroke, or something that changes your situation in life, and it can happen in an instant. In this situation, you or a family member may suffer bodily harm and require long-term care.

You may have a family member in a perpetual coma.

Someone may become blind, deaf, or crippled.

Someone may develop terminal cancer and now face the long path to death.

Someone may have a life-threatening disease that leaves the body physically stricken for the rest of its life.

When something happens that creates traumatic, shocking, sickening change, you go through the same grief reactions emotionally, physically, and spiritually as a death in the family. The world you took for granted is no more. Not only do you have to grieve it, but you also have to face the sense of insecurity that follows. What happens next? Will I or he or she get better? Will things ever be the same? No, things cannot ever be the same, and that will have to be grieved, too.

Life is only about change. Mortal life is designed to offer varied and interesting experiences of every single type. This design can definitely include a change in your life. For example, if you are a soldier and have lost a limb in battle, you are going to grieve that your body has changed. You know that you will be changing emotionally. You become concerned about how others—family and friends—will react. There is such a flood of emotion that you almost cannot sort it out fast enough. Then you come face-to-face with the physical pain and the physical therapy. It is very much an uphill battle. The loss of independence alone is profoundly disheartening. This is the same emotional scenario whether or not you develop breast cancer, go blind, or become a paraplegic or a quadriplegic.

Every catastrophic thing that happens to you is disheartening at first. It does not have to remain that way. How you live out the rest of your life will depend on your motivation to live and to grow. Some of the most powerful lessons anyone has ever had came through these types of experiences.

There is an opportunity here, as in all the other situations, to heal yourself. Everything changes, whether you want it to or not. Doing whatever you can to maintain continuity in your life is healing. Above all, you must be kind and patient with yourself. You must allow yourself to grieve. Through counseling you may learn to change your attitude to one of gratitude for the opportunity to grow that this experience has offered. Allow a down day occasionally; then take heart and live this life all the way.

Change in Life Situation — Physical Surroundings

Fires, floods, tornados, earthquakes, volcanic eruptions, revolutions—all are astounding things that can cause you to lose everything that you have ever owned: home, car, property, way of life, and income. There is also the death from financial disaster through job loss, foreclosure, and bankruptcy. There is attachment to all these things, and the destruction of that attachment creates grief. This is a unique type of grief. Even though it was just a job, or a dwelling, or just so much photography, or so much ceramic, it was yours. The loss of a job is a huge loss of personal identity. The loss of every piece of art, clothing, picture, plate, and brick represents a precious memory. Each time you looked at the item, the memory was returned to you, and you felt it. Once destroyed, it is as if part of your life was also destroyed at the same time, and there is just no replacing it. Emptiness takes its place. You begin the natural process of grieving this loss.

If the loss is through foreclosure or bankruptcy, the grief not only of the loss but also of the personal humiliation and shame of having to ask family, friends and neighbors for help and of being unable to financially manage your life is tremendous. There may also be the powerful grief associated with the loss of a job or of a position. Many angry people have taken their "grief" out on their employers through violent means.

The best way to deal with this loss is to talk about it. Work through the resultant anger, and, then, be grateful for what you can. Maybe a home was lost, but the family and pets were saved. Perhaps you lost your job, home, and even a car, but your family is intact; your family is helping you, and you are starting on a major life change. Maybe a country's government fell, but all family members who either lived there or were stationed there were able to leave the country safely. Accept that you are going to have to do the grief work and begin the process.

Look for the reason it happened, look for the lessons, and begin to understand that once you leave the physical plane, all those things will be left behind in the natural course of events. Perhaps yours is the lesson of letting go of attachment early and learning how to heal. There may also be the lesson of understanding profound change in your life and learning to heal yourself. Whatever the lesson is, it will be a valuable one that will help you to understand the bigger picture.

Misconstrued Concepts of Death

We have many preconceived notions of what death is. Our culture views discussing death as morbid, sad, unsavory, dark, depressing, and unnecessary. We believe that death is something to be feared—that it is a great tragedy and, most importantly, that it is permanent. These notions are created in many places, and whether stemming from society, religion, or basic fear of the unknown, they are just that—notions. There is no validity to these ideas. Such beliefs and concepts of death and the afterlife greatly retard our spiritual progression while we are here on Earth.

The symbols of death are imbedded in our subconscious from the black-hooded "Grim Reaper" holding a vicious-looking scythe to a grinning skeleton holding its own skull. The macabre terrifies us with its blood, gore, mutilation, and horror. Even fairy tales are full of terrible ways to die, and we read these to our children as we send them off to sleep.

With such iconoclastic representations of death, what emotion other than fear could the very word *death* create in our minds? Even religions, the very institutions designed to bring us peace, have viewed death and the afterlife as a means of control. Fear of death and all that surrounds it keeps people in line. Feelings of guilt and fear of punishment maintain this control.

Another concept concerning death is the tragedy of it all. People die, and we put them in the ground, bury them at sea, or cremate them. We cry, wail, or bury our feelings of loss, sometimes of such profound loss that there can be no consolation. But what if it is not a bad event? What if death is not a tragedy? The belief that death is a tragedy stems from the fear that surrounds it and the misguided notion that it is permanent.

Where does this conception of tragedy come from? Perhaps it comes from the mistaken belief that the last breath is permanent. The last breath *is* permanent but only for that lifetime. Of course there will be sadness associated with this event. However, understanding that death is the end of this particular mortal life and is only the end of this phase of this soul's cycle may begin to remove the sense of tragedy surrounding someone's passing.

Perhaps the death of another reminds you of your own mortality. Perhaps people feel that they will never, ever see this beloved person again. The false permanence of death causes people to fear the loss of their own identity, believing that at the moment of death they will simply cease to be. You learned earlier, however, that energy moves in cycles. The end of one cycle is the beginning of another. The energy that animates the human form moves in that cycle. When the body dies, the energy enters a different phase of the cycle but will eventually return to this phase again. Ultimately this awareness is the foundation for the understanding of reincarnation. You live a life and you die. You move into the heaven world; you learn from this last mortal life, and you are then reborn.

We are all going to experience death. In this process, there are certain times when we are presented with specific things called death gates from where it may be easier to begin that transition to the heaven world than at other times.

Death Gates

A death gate is literally a doorway in our life that occurs when we may be unconsciously contemplating leaving mortal life. A death gate can be a time period or an event. Sometimes it can be both a time and an event such as an accident or illness. Virtually everyone experiences these gates, but few are aware of them. (An example is the person who has a close call and takes decisive action to stop a bad situation.) People seldom have any awareness of the presence of death gates. They just know that there were times in their life when they actually felt that they could die and choose not to physically leave.

Death gates are presented to us throughout our lives. We encounter a death gate with every birthday we have. Those gates pass harmlessly enough most of the time, but a surprising number of people die within thirty days before or after their birthday. The reason these gates seem to occur around a person's birthday is possibly because mortal life and physical death are part of the cycle of life. We find that people often end life around the time when life began.

What is the purpose of a death gate? Often the purpose of a death gate is to offer us an opportunity to decide to stay and work through the unique challenges that this life offers. A death gate could be considered an unconscious emotional milestone. Quite a few of us can think back to particularly perilous moments when we could surely have died. There was much drama associated with each situation. If careful analysis is given to each time, much can be learned. For instance, if people have a terrible sickness in their childhoods, perhaps they were not happy with their parents. If they were in a single car accident, perhaps they just did not want to be here anymore. If some people have suffered terribly at the hands of a vicious parent, perhaps their scarlet fever was the rage they were never allowed to express. The fever could kill them, scar them, or make them stronger. Sometimes a death gate occurs when people want to test themselves. Literally, they just see how close they can come to death; these are the dare devil's among us. All are choices, both conscious and subconscious, that we each make.

As a critical exercise, you would be wise to think back to every serious, life–threatening illness or event you have ever experienced. Gently, with compassion for your family and yourself, think back to what was happening to you at those times. What were the circumstances? Were you angry, depressed, fearful, guilt–ridden, grief–stricken, tired of the pain, filled with hate or rage? What was going on? Your illnesses or accidents are a method of communication from your subconscious. Sometimes people have no other way to voice what their deepest feelings are except through accidents and illness. Sadly, few people are able to translate those illnesses or accidents into meaningful words the conscious mind can understand. The emotional energy of a situation or event has to go somewhere, and frequently it manifests in accidents and illnesses.

Death can be a conscious or unconscious decision to leave. The following are examples of the unconscious decision: If you almost die from a raging fever and you decide to stay and fight back, did you change your mind about leaving? Medical histories are replete with stories of people who, technically or mechanically, should not be alive, but they are. They chose to continue life in a physical body rather than returning to the heaven world. Many people die from things that should never have killed them; medical histories are full of these cases, too. Some people die, and there is absolutely no explanation; they just leave. "No cause of death determined" is listed on the death certificate. Families are filled with bewildered grief at those situations.

What about people who endure tremendous hardship and yet never seem to get sick or have an accident? Are there death gates for them, as well? Of course, we all have moments when we are tested. How did some amazing souls survive the numerous holocausts that have happened to people worldwide? Perhaps in these situations, they just closed the doors of those death gates. Suicide is a case in which someone literally walks through those death gates. Even for those who commit suicide, though, there is no end—just a new beginning in another realm.

There Is No End

Many thousands of writers have sought to explain that there is no ceasing of life. Life cannot die. Life will always continue in some other form. Just because you cannot see that form does not mean that it does not exist. The word "death" implies an end, but it is simply a doorway to another form of existence. The concept "in your Father's House are many mansions" truly means that you literally have a choice as to which mansion door you will enter. This is basic physics, and it is perhaps the most fundamental element of faith that any person can have.

It is always curious to observe that, when a person ceases to use his or her physical body for whatever the reason, those, who love and grieve that personality, often lose their faith in the very spiritual and physical process of life, literally, *being* itself. In other words, life just keeps changing its form. This isn't good or bad; it just is. Faith in God and in the wonder of the divine should not be lost in the waves of grief that sweep those left behind.

The point here is that you never die; you just change energy forms. Your thoughts are still your thoughts. Your feelings and emotions are still there. The difference is that now you exist purely through your thoughts. You are not feeling the physical body; you are experiencing only your thoughts. The energy of who you are is still there. The energy of life continues beyond the death of the physical body. The body just carries you through the experiences of living. The soul is eternal. Imagine, if you could know this before your death, how much more peaceful your life would be!

Past Lives, Reincarnation, Life Everlasting

You live thousands of lives to gain experiences. As you reincarnate, a veil comes down, and all memory of past lives is lost, but familiarity with people, places, and things persists. A veil is literally an energetic boundary between the mortal realm and the immortal realm. The veil or boundary is necessary so that you will have an absolutely new and unique opportunity for necessary experiences as you embark on each new incarnation. You remember what you need to remember to work through new lessons or try to come to terms with old ones. If you did not resolve a situation in one life, you get to come back and try again. The typical reincarnation cycle is believed to be 152 years, but souls have come back in as few as 5 years. People return to live again and again. This is why people, places, and things are familiar; you have experienced them before.

The concept of reincarnation is the essence of the idea of *life everlasting*. It is the thought that there is no death—only transition. It is also the concept that you are here for soul evolution, for service in this and every life. *Reincarnation* is just another term for the cycle of life and death.

You choose life. You choose your eventual death as part of the normal cycle of life. You even unconsciously choose the method of death. You choose this returning-home method to leave the pain or lessons of the Earth plane. Sometimes it is so very hard to live day-to-day that staying on the Earth plane is more than a particular soul can bear.

Sometimes, you experience an early death as a particular lesson, and sometimes the particular lesson is whether or not to choose death and then to stay and endure in order to learn, grow, and evolve. Death is an extremely important aspect of soul evolution. An example is the story of the woman, who, through several past life regressions, discovered that she had lost the same loved one, life after life. Each time he died, she decided that she could not live without him, so she killed herself to be with him. Finally, in one life, a variation of the same scenario occurred, and she was able to live, marry, and find happiness after the death of this soul. This is an outstanding example of soul evolution.

Compassion for the choices each soul makes is one of the best ways to deal with death. Compassion for yourself as well as for the person who leaves is a critical element of healing and of your own soul evolution. Your continuing evolution is the key element of your understanding of reincarnation. Acknowledging reincarnation provides critical understanding of the life and death process. In his book *The Place We Call Home*, Robert J. Grant explains:

> The cycles of life and death, from earthly life to the unseen worlds, are preparation for a higher calling, a higher form of creation that the soul is becoming. It isn't possible for each soul to unfold and become like its Creator in one small life span on Earth. It is a gradual unfoldment, an evolution through time and space, and many, many lives.[1]

If we could all accept that we cannot destroy a soul—souls are immortal and infinite—then we could begin to grasp why we are here, what we may learn from our experiences, and how we can help others.

Death would not be as filled with grief and guilt. Few people allow a loved one to return to the heaven world without experiencing some anger, guilt, or remorse toward that person. If these kinds of emotions could be avoided or at least understood, then, perhaps, the process of transition could be less painful for all those involved in the death of a loved one. It is important that we objectively evaluate our relationships, removing any guilt and replacing it with the understanding of the purpose of a life. This will yield far more progress in soul evolution for all parties. It is comforting to remember that nothing kills a soul; souls are eternal. We all return home to God.

Perchance, as we ponder these deeper concepts of death, it would be wise to consider that, no matter what we think we are seeing when a person is killed, nothing kills a soul. Accidents, knives, bombs, bullets, poison, pills, fire, water, and disease are merely methods of transferring soul personality from one form to another. We all have to die of something. We will all eventually shed this physical body for another one.

Human beings almost always ask about the cause of death when they hear that someone has passed away. "How did this person die?" we ask, anxiously hoping that somehow we will be immune from that particular cause of death. Perhaps we secretly hope that somehow we will be immortal and the process of death will forget about us. Someone else's death reminds us that no one is immune. The richly famous and the powerfully mean souls will have the same rendezvous with death as the merely mortal and the angelically blessed ones among us.

No matter the terrible things that happen, the only constant in life is the ever-changing form of life energy. Life's longing for expression manifests in endless opportunities for all types of unique experiences. If a baby dies, the soul of this child will return in another time and in another place. A soldier killed in battle will return to live again. Elderly people will return in fresh new bodies to seek to learn what was not learned as they left their tired old bodies. Death is never the end of a soul. Death is merely the end of one experience and the doorway to another one. We cannot destroy the energy of a soul. The flow of life is the flow of the waters of energy, constantly changing form, always returning in one form or another in this cycle called mortal life.

What defines how you live each life and what experiences you will have is something called karma.

Karma

Karma is the concept that everything you do comes back to you. Remember the golden rule? *Do unto others, as you would have them do unto you.* This concept exists in every faith in this world. What you cause another to experience, you will, in turn, eventually experience. This is what helps you sleep at night. If someone does something negative or hurtful, this energy or these actions will be returned to that person in some manner. Karma balances all things. Conversely, as you do something wonderful for another person, the energy of that good deed will be returned to you in some appropriate manner at another point in time. Even if the other person does not acknowledge it, the energy of your good deeds has to come back to you. This is also a key element in spiritual law. It is how you handle these experiences that helps you to evolve as a person and as a soul.

The beauty of karma lies in its infinite opportunity. Many, many people at the point of death realize that they have led, shall we say, quite checkered lives. They find that they are not always proud of how they lived their lives, often wishing that they could have done so many things differently. They review their choices and find a focus on money instead of relationship or on ambition and questionable fame instead of building a foundation of gratifying morals and ethics. The point of death for some souls can be a time to work on purifying their karma by literally being genuinely sorry for the life they have led. If they are fortunate enough to be able to know that they are dying and to ask for forgiveness from those they may have harmed and to forgive those who may have harmed them; then, in those precious moments of enlightenment, atonement can begin.

For those who have led lives of service, love, and overall happiness, they can expand their karmic appreciation by sending powerful energies of love as a way of helping those who will grieve them.

The moment of death is exceptionally powerful because you are coming to terms with yourself. If the death is sudden, there may not be the same opportunity for this understanding. However, if you know that you are dying and are genuinely sorry for any hurt you caused others, it can make a powerful difference in how the karma will be returned in the next life. Not all the karma you accumulate in each life can be returned to you in each life. Sometimes, it takes lifetimes for all of it to come back, but it does come back. This is why each moment of mortal life and death is so pregnant with consequences. There is always a consequence to what you do and how you handle each situation life presents.

In Charles Dickens' *A Christmas Carol*, Mr. Scrooge was actually shown his karmic life. He saw his childhood, the experiences he had, and the lessons he learned. He also saw the lessons he could have learned and how these lessons created in him a miserly attitude toward his fellow man. He was able to see how and when his heart was closed off and how the choices he made affected all of those around him. Mr. Scrooge was so emotionally closed to the needs and feelings of others that it took a tremendous amount of work for him to understand finally that he was here to learn the lessons of love and that the more he shut down, the more the karma he created was literally shutting him off from the whole world. He was also shown how his karmic actions affected other people. He was given an opportunity before his eventual death to change his future karmic actions. He was truly sorry for what he had become and how he had hurt other people. In those precious moments of understanding, he began to change his karmic path. You can do the same if you can understand the significance of how your actions today will echo out into your future.

As Mr. Scrooge sought to change his karmic path through good deeds, he found that he had to ask people to forgive his previous, often cruel, actions. He found that he was also ashamed of himself. At some point Mr. Scrooge and all of us have to forgive ourselves. So on this karmic path to spiritual growth, we must come face-to-face with the power of forgiveness, both for ourselves and for those around us.

Not all people get to understand the karmic fabric of their lives. Sometimes a soul gets to understand life only through its own death. Every death has a purpose for the one transitioning to the heaven world and for those loved ones left behind. The lessons of love and understanding can be life changing.

The Purpose of Death

Every single death has a purpose. No one dies without there being a meaning to that person's death. If someone you love dies, you endlessly ask for answers: Why did this person leave now, in this way? Why?

The purpose of every death is to teach you lessons about love. The myriad forms of this lesson are why there are so many types of death at so many different ages. If every person died after 100 years of living, if every life were exactly the same, then what would be learned? Nothing. The very sameness with which life was lived would be extremely detrimental. It is the surprising occurrence and the astonishing array of methods of death that teach you so much. This may be a very difficult concept to accept, for the dynamic of dying is as precious a concept as the dynamic of living.

What if you cannot readily understand the reason that someone you loved, were close to, or even saw on TV died? The very fact that you asked the question is evidence that you are thinking on higher levels. Ask questions, and then listen patiently for the answers.

Sometimes the answers teach you to value life or teach you how little others value life. Some deaths teach you the lessons of cruelty and the lessons of hope. Some deaths offer you the opportunity to forgive and to heal. All death is an opportunity for the person dying and for those left behind to learn. For the dying, it is the final lesson on the Earth plane. For the living, it is an opportunity to live life differently with more awareness and, ever hopefully, more love.

As you view this study on the end of a life, look always for the lessons of love and compassion. It is not gross or morbid to want to understand death. Understanding all the aspects of death will enable you to open your heart more to others. The often dormant seeds of compassion may be sprouted within you. Learning all you can about death will remove much fear, trepidation, and pain. With a death, some of the most poignant lessons come from the process of grieving. As you learn to love more through the process of understanding death, you can be of much greater service to your friends and family. You can learn to use more frequently the power of prayer to send healing to anyone anywhere who needs love and care. You can help. When you can learn compassion for others through a death, you will have grown as a soul, for you will have learned to love more. Hopefully, what you are able to provide to others will end up being the very elements of compassion that you will eventually want for yourself, no matter what the situation.

The Concept of Embracing Death

What does it mean to embrace death? It means to cease the fear of death, the horror of it. You embrace death when you can accept the fact that when people die and their physical bodies cease to function, their souls are not destroyed. The souls are just in a different dimension.

You embrace death when you do not cling to people who are dying, begging them to get better when it really is time for them to transition to the heaven world.

You embrace death by allowing the soul of the person who has died to leave and to move on into the heaven world. People who refuse to release their loved one delay that soul's transition to the heaven world.

You embrace death when you seek to understand the nature of dying and rebirth and when you learn to understand the cycle of soul evolution.

You embrace death when you can begin to imagine that your beloved is in a wonderful place, is not in pain, is not afraid, and is living in joy.

You embrace death when you can understand that your loved one is no longer grieving his or her own passing and is no longer grieving you. You recognize that your beloved is not grieving because he or she is feeling the happiness of divine light and love.

You embrace death when you can gently and lovingly nudge yourself out of the way and decide to be happy for your loved one because you finally understand *that this person's life was complete at the time of his or her death.* He or she did not need another 50 or 90 or 2 more years to have a complete life. The soul received everything he or she needed—all the lessons he or she came for in the exact amount of time lived. When that time was finished, the soul returned to its real home.

You embrace death when you finally acknowledge that not everyone needs 100 years of life. This is a huge step because maybe before, while you might have been able to understand it for someone else, it was an inconceivable concept when applied to your own son or daughter, mom or dad, or friend or pet. Now it is a reality for you, and you have reached a place of peaceful understanding.

Mostly, you grieve not for the souls who have died but for yourself. It is you who must deal with death and must come to release those who leave their bodies. You must release your own fears of death. When someone dies, you come face-to-face with your own mortality, thinking death is the end, but souls are not destroyed. Often you dare not think too much of this place for fear that it is not real, but it is real. It is wonderful, and it is whatever you make of it. You cease your fear death by:

- Welcoming the next stage of soul evolution.
- Recognizing that death is returning to God.
- Remembering that you will see all whom you love again and again.
- Releasing your fear of judgment, for God does not judge you; you judge yourself.
- Releasing your fear of God, for it is not He who creates your pain; you do.
- Releasing your fear of the heaven world, for it is a place of joy.
- Transmuting your fear by replacing it with love and joy for life in any dimension in which you may live.

The wonderful part of all of this is that the more you can be comfortable with the concepts of mortal life transition, what you call death, the more you can look forward to embracing your own entrance into the heaven world when that day inevitably comes.

2

Concepts of Grief

For life and death are one, and only those who will consider the experience as one may come to understand or comprehend what peace indeed means.

Edgar Cayce Reading 1977

The Utter Uniqueness and Aloneness of Grief

No one has ever felt such an ever constant aching in their heart as I am feeling. There is a sense of aloneness to how I feel, an emptiness. Why does the sun go on shining? Doesn't the sun know how bad I feel? Can't anyone make this terrible feeling, this pain, just go away? I can't believe that I will ever feel normal again.

I can't believe my body can hold this many tears; they keep coming at the most inappropriate times. Do they have to keep playing that favorite song or the most painful song in the world every time I turn my radio on? I used to love to cook. What's the use now? Everything reminds me of her—the scent of her clothes, the things or toys she used. Oh, God, the photographs! Everywhere I look I am haunted. Laundry is so hard, washing away her memories. How am I supposed to do that?

I am in pain. I ache all over. I really don't want to hear about the death of someone else's dog or dad or mom or relative or, or, or any more sadness! How can there possibly be so much sadness?

People avoid my eyes or gaze. They don't call. It is just as well—no one ever knows what to say anyway. What is there to say? "How am I?" "Oh, I'm fine," I say, but inside I feel horrible. I hate lying. But I can't say, "I feel like I am dying inside, and that feeling just keeps lingering and lingering. I just want to scream and escape myself so I won't have to keep feeling this pain!"

I consider dying myself, but I can't bring myself to do this to someone else. There is an emptiness that just cannot seem to be filled. It is as if the love lights went out in my life. I want to turn them back on and be the same person, but I just can't find the match or the switch or the will inside me to go back to being who I was. Who I was died with her. Now, somehow, I am someone else, and I really don't know this person—I don't know myself anymore. I need an introduction to this person in the mirror; this person doesn't know how to live and cannot find a path out of the darkness.

I have to do all those stupid mundane things like grocery shop or return gifts I bought for her because she just can't use this piece of jewelry or doll or dress. I have to go back to my everyday world and choke back this tidal wave feeling that haunts me day and night. Can't anyone make this terrible feeling go away?

I am also grieving myself! I will never be the same again! I miss the old me!

People try to help me; they are well-meaning but clearly clueless. Nothing they say helps. Occasionally someone knows, but that person is rare. I actually avoid this person because he or she really knows my heart and that could be dangerous—I just might let the dam of real emotion explode, and what good would that do? Grief is agony. Is it over yet? Please, God, let this be over so I can be me again. . .

Grief

When someone you love dies or something important to you ends, there is a part of you that feels as though your heart has been broken into a thousand pieces. You are so bewildered by the profound power of these emotions that it is often hard to find your balance. This new energy that is grief demands your attention every moment, never leaving you until you begin to do the work to get to the other side of it. It is as if you have a new shadow self and that self is grief. That grief shadow is that part of you that needs healing after any trauma you may experience. No matter how you define it, you will come to understand that grief, as much as it is an emotion, is also a process of healing.

Grief is also a process of releasing attachment, of transmuting your emotional connections to people, places, or things, and of eventually finding a way to heal yourself. When you are plunged into a grieving process, you cling desperately to what you have that still connects you to that person, place, or situation. Eventually you will have to let go of that attachment. It will be important to understand the myriad elements of attachment, how they affect you, and what you can do to begin to release your attachments. Releasing attachments is a critical step in healing not only your own shattered heart but also the hearts of those grieving around you.

Grief is change. Grief is the process of accepting the fact that something in your life has ended and will never be the same. Grief is processing the emotions that go with this change. Because change is a constant, you are continually required to embrace the new while learning to let go of the old. When a death occurs, you are seldom prepared to handle all that will be required of you now. Just as with a burned forest, it is hard for you to realize that amongst the embers of your charred heart are the seeds of tomorrow's healing for your grieving heart.

As you go through your life, you will encounter many, many things to grieve. Some people even grieve the end of an era or a way of life. Everyone is grieving something. Throughout your life you are given many initiations into the various facets of grief so that you can learn how to grieve with grace. If you choose to learn this lesson, then you may be of greater service to others who have not recognized those initiations and learned those lessons. Eventually, you come to the concept of healing grief through service.

Understanding the end of something is also an opportunity to understand how many facets there actually are to grief. Even the dead grieve their own passing in many circumstances. There are many types of death, and grief accompanies them all. Understanding this will enable you to be of greater service when you can and to help you grow in spiritual understanding during this endless cycle of life and death.

The Demands to Know Why the Person Died and "*Why Did This Happen to Me?*"

Why did my child die?

Why did my husband leave me with all these kids?

How could my mom or dad die so early? I'm only 4 or 5 or 30.

What was my best friend thinking when he or she committed suicide?

What does it mean: They had something else to do? Where? Why?

Why did this person die —now? Why?

Why am I divorced, or disabled, or paralyzed?

Why did my house burn down?

Every single person who has ever had a life crisis has asked this question a hundred times: How could this possibly have happened?

There are many possible answers, but the only one that universally applies is so that you can have the experience of this event, no matter how traumatic. It is the collection of experiences you have in each life and how you respond to those experiences that define you and take you either to a new place of growth or to a place of darkness.

Nothing is a punishment. Everything is an experience for your greater good. Sometimes profound adversity offers you some of your greatest opportunities to discover your strength and courage. Many times, you look back and wonder how you managed to get to the other side of very difficult situations. If you can accept that the situation happened and that you can grow from the lessons learned in that experience, you may be able to avoid the next most common feeling after a death which is anger at God.

Anger at God

It does not matter how you define your faith. It does not matter whether you go to any church or have any religious beliefs whatsoever. When a massive trauma occurs, there is an almost instantaneous response of wanting to blame someone for what has happened. There are those situations when someone just dies, or you are just ill, or something just happens, and there is *no one to blame*. So you call the event an *act of God*. This phrase makes it really easy to blame God for the situation. Even if there is supposedly someone or something to blame, you still become angry with God.

The truth is that sometimes events happen. You just have to accept this fact and learn to heal. But accepting what has happened in your life is a really courageous act, and often when you are alone, in pain, and depressed, you have to be angry with someone, and so you pick God.

God does not give anyone pain. You may not always know why you have a particular experience; you just know that now you are faced with a very difficult future. How you choose to handle the experience given to you is what will define your future both in this life and the next. You have known people who have experienced a death or other life trauma, and they allowed their reaction to the event to ruin their lives forever. You know that you are never going to be the same after any experience. The experience becomes a force of change that molds you. The challenge is to make this experience something that enables you to grow. There are other people who take the experience, honor it through their own grieving process, and then continue to honor the person who died or the trauma they had by somehow making the world a better place. You choose how you will react. You have a choice to be happy or sad. Telling yourself that you will never be happy again is a terrible sentence because that sentence is not yours alone. You do not live in a vacuum.

When you choose to be angry with God and to never heal, you sentence all those around you—family, friends, co-workers, bosses, and employees—to continually experience your pain with you. Misery loves company. The people around you, in turn, don't really heal either, and the ripple effect of this endless anger and pain just keeps echoing through the years.

The hardest task and the most accelerated methods of healing are to accept responsibility for your life and to decide to heal. Neither God nor anyone can heal you unless you choose to heal and to move forward. Horrible things do happen to very good people. It is the process of healing yourself that will define you for the next thousand years.

Each experience is an opportunity for emotional and spiritual growth or emotional and spiritual death. You must choose your path. Whatever you choose, be aware that it will affect literally hundreds of people around you as your choice reverberates through the lives of other

people. No matter what has happened, rise to a higher level and heal—
the consequences will be miraculous.

Tears for the Dead

Why do you grieve those who have died? You cry at funerals for your
loss. It is your sadness in knowing that you will never see them again,
never hold, hug, touch, or be with the ones you loved. You may find
that you are often grieving yourself and for who you were with that
person. You are a new person now, and you have to adjust to a whole
new life.

Crying is an action that releases much emotion both for the changes
in your life and for the person who has gone. That type of crying is
actually a good action. That crying honors your love and your beloved.
Yet even this mourning would be short if you knew what grand realities
and wondrous experiences await the joyous soul leaving the body.

You may decide to grieve the lost relationship with your loved one
that can now never be the same, but it is also important to honor the
new life that your beloved is now experiencing and to acknowledge
that his or her experience in the heaven world is wonderful. It can be
most helpful to maintain an awareness of your loved one in the heaven
world. This can be a crucial element in healing your grief. Remembering their wonderful passage through the realms of the heaven world
may shorten your journey through the various stages of grief.

Waves of Grief

When news of a death hits you, there is the initial feeling that a tidal
wave of emotion has just struck you. Depending on the relationship
you had with the person who has died or the event, such as a divorce or
loss of home and property or physical function, there is a virtual up-
heaval to your very foundation. This crisis creates a continuing echo of
waves of emotion that can last for a long time.

This echo of emotion comes at you in the form of a wave of grief. This
wave can hit you no matter where you are, what you are doing, or
whom you are with. It is crippling at first, reducing you to tears and

depression for minutes, or hours, or—for some, sadly—days and weeks. You can eventually come out of the effects. The distance between the waves is the measure of progress in healing your grief.

The waves of grief can come with no warning or can be triggered by a song, a color, a smell, an object, or something that the person wore or said or would have done. Often you feel this wave of emotion when you realize that the life you expected to have with this person or home or situation will now not ever take place. That expectation has been changed forever, and accepting this fact will be very challenging. Your task is to adjust to this realization, and being able to handle the grief wave is the method by which you adjust. Denying the emotions you feel will lead only to physical problems.

When the wave hits, if it is really inappropriate to cry in front of someone, then excuse yourself and release this emotion in a restroom, if necessary. While this may not be the location of choice, it is much better than keeping emotion bottled up all the time. You can cry in the shower, letting the warm water comfort you and wash away the tears. Bathing away the grief is a balanced form of healing. You can call some-one with whom you are totally comfortable and ask that the person just listen for a bit as you are experiencing a moment of grief. You can go ahead and cry. Fear of tears is unnecessary. You have the ability to cry for a reason. Tears are the mechanism for the release of emotion. It is normal to put on a brave face for the public part of your life, but it is not okay to keep that face in place in private. You are wise when you release your grief and then rest. Grieving is exhausting. It is important to give yourself permission to take extra rest. Sometimes you cannot differentiate between what is the actual exhausting energy of grieving and what is depression. The line between the two is very fine. The more rest you have, the more you can differentiate between grieving and depression, because you will have better judgment when you are better rested. You may find that you cry, rest, and then just keep going. This is the physical process of healing.

Religion

What role has religion played in the process of healing grief?

Everyone's religious experience is different when it comes to grief. Some religious leaders offer meaningless platitudes to the grieving families and tell them that they will heal in time. Many do try to help, but often even they do not explain some of the more esoteric aspects of death. Learning about these more unusual elements that make death understandable may not be within the purview of many religious leaders.

Whatever your religious background, it is worthwhile to evaluate whether or not there is a fixation on sin. Some groups believe that we are all sinners and that God punishes us. Some believe that God sees the sins you commit and will hold you accountable on Judgment Day. Some people are taught to believe that they aren't good enough to go to heaven. If they are not baptized or "saved," then they will go straight to hell, with no chance at heaven; even their innocence or service to mankind would not apply. This type of philosophy does not offer the grieving person any sense of compassion or healing.

No wonder we have so many distraught ghosts troubling the living! They were not only terrified of the physical process of dying, but they were also afraid of what would happen to their souls after they left their bodies. The thought of God's judgment is especially terrifying for many of them. Many people wonder why ghosts don't move toward the light even when it comes. Frequently, dead people do not feel they are worthy of God's love and, therefore, are not worthy of the light. Some souls are so full of guilt that they create their very own cold and empty afterlives. This information has been told to intuitives who assist the ghosts who have committed suicide or died in accidents or in other types of violent and non-violent deaths. What kind of a God would cause such fear in His children? Why would the idea of a loving God be reserved only for the truly deserving? These concepts are especially tortuous for grieving relatives. If their loved one committed suicide, they believe that this soul may have no chance for redemption. If a child dies before being baptized, the family may feel that their child is not pure enough to enter the realm of God. If their loved one was very troubled, this feeling of not knowing that the person they are grieving can be loved by God is especially cruel. It is important to remember that God loves all souls. Hopefully, we can all embrace a religious belief with this kind and compassionate philosophy.

It is always wise to remember that God sends His love equally, for all beings in all faiths: sinners, saints, and the ordinary person. How does He do this? He gives us the same sun that shines on all of us, and the same nourishing rains that wash our lands without discrimination. The concept of a compassionate God invites you to relinquish judgment. When you stop judging others, you free yourself to see them as children of a loving God and to accept that something has happened in their lives to make them the way they are. Sometimes you just have to accept what you cannot change. This is especially true after a death. Wishing that a loved one had been different or had gone to church will not help either the grieving person or the departed soul to heal. It is wise to remember that as each person prays, he or she is praying to a loving and compassionate God.

God Never Punishes Us: Understanding That Everything Happens in Perfect Order

Even though this is profoundly difficult to believe, all karma is exquisitely fair.

All death happens in perfect order, even though your mortal world feels like chaos.

All events take place for your higher good, even though the pain you are experiencing seems interminable.

When someone you love dies or a relationship of any kind ends, this is part of the divine plan, even though you cannot see it or understand it now.

All seemingly broken hearts can heal—*all of them*—when each soul can look at the event as just that: an event for one's higher good. Look for the answer; look for the reason. Cease judgment of the event as either good or bad. This course will accelerate spiritual growth and healing faster than any other action. This action will cool anger and pain. Railing against God that what has occurred is not fair or right or just or sensible will not help you to see the higher good. Look for the reason; look for the benefit; gently place your ego out of the way, and look at the bigger picture. While this may seem hard to do at first, it is the surest way to reach that place of healing.

Some people feel that a dark cloud has followed them and that they are being punished by this grief. This is not so. All karma is exquisitely fair, perfect in every way, designed for your maximum benefit—designed so that you can open your heart to all that is. So what does this mean? Perhaps it means that every experience is designed for you to learn from. Learning the lessons from every experience, no matter how hard, enables you to grow as a person, enables you to have an understanding of what, for example, grief is. Once you have opened your heart to understanding grief, then, perhaps, you can open your heart to others who are grieving and possibly reach out to them, as well. Perhaps, now, you can understand what your co-worker felt when his or her mom or sister or even a precious pet died. Now you know. Now you can open your compassionate heart to them, as well. The death or sadness that you have experienced will have become a precious lesson for you, and you can use this knowledge to help or to be compassionate to all whom you may meet. Everyone has a story. Everyone is grieving someone or something.

Hence, it is important to understand that among the hardest things is trusting that what has occurred, no matter how painful, is an event designed to empower you, to help you to grow, and to provide service to others because of your greater level of insight.

3

STAGES OF GRIEVING

It is not all of life, then, to live, nor all of death to die; but
what the entity [person] does *with* the opportunities as they
present themselves.   Edgar Cayce Reading 2630-1

There are numerous stages of grief. Every person who writes about
grief lists the stages. They are longer or shorter for each person,
and each person's experience is unique. This list is not all-inclu-
sive, but it does help you understand what you, or someone you
love, may be experiencing.

Disbelief, Shock, and Numbness

You receive the word that someone you love has died, or that
you are getting divorced, or that your house has been hit by a
tornado. *"No, this cannot be true. Oh, God, this cannot be happening!"* As
you begin to go through the torture of living through the day-
after-day events, you are actually helped along by the adrenaline
in your body and by those around you who are supporting you.
You mechanically go through the motions of doing the initially
required actions.

Numbness in its own humble way is a blessing because it allows you to get through those unbelievably hard moments of picking out a casket or deciding on burial plans. It enables you to tell loved ones the difficult news and yet still hold yourself together with some level of dignity. It makes it possible for you to meet people and to put on a brave face even though inside you may want to go somewhere and hide.

You will someday look back and ask yourself how you ever got through that time. Numbness got you through that time. You know that you were numb with shock. Eventually, however, the numbness and shock wear off, and you are swept up with a whole new set of emotions. For some people, this is denial.

Denial

This cannot be true! This isn't what I planned! This isn't really happening to me. Surely, surely, oh please, let me wake up and know that this was only some horrible dream!

She isn't really dead. I am still married. My house is still there. They will walk through the door—the door will still be there.

Sleep is torture. I must find a way not to wake up. If this is true, how can I live?

Never speaking of a person is an aspect of denial. Some families forbid even the mention of someone who passed from their lives. This form of denial sets up a toxic energy in everyone's body. In this case, denial never ends. Some people never leave the denial stage.

Some people cross the very fine line between sanity and fantasy. The death or tragic event is so tremendous that the individual slips into a fantasy world of manufactured reality. In this other world, the deceased person is still there. The grief-stricken person can still talk to the deceased and is not sad. If a person is in a fragile state to begin with, this loss can push him or her across this subtle line. Family and friends cannot reach the bereaved. In severe cases, the person in the denial stage moves not into anger but into severe depression and finds that suicide is the ultimate answer.

For the more balanced person, as the truth sets in, a chilling reality hits him or her. If this is happening, you may find that along with the severe heartache, there is a desire to deny all the follow-on realities that go with a life crisis. This means that you do not want to move forward in a world that has changed so radically.

Most often, true denial is a time when the people or events are never spoken of; their pictures are put away; their room is sealed off. Denial is a false feeling of containing pain, but eventually, that pain surfaces. Sometimes when you allow the denial to end, the anger begins.

Anger and Punishment

How can this be happening? I am so angry at everything and everyone. I just want to scream! There must be someone responsible for the horrible way I feel. Why am I being punished? What in the world did I ever do to anyone to deserve this pain?

I am angry at the cause of my pain.

I am angry at the loss of my loved one, or home, or life.

I am angry with God for letting this happen to me.

I am angry with myself for being in this position in the first place.

I am angry at their choice of not taking better care of themselves, of choosing to die this way.

I am angry with all the happy people around me—How dare they have such seemingly perfect lives? Tell me again why I am being punished so?

I am angry that life is just so seemingly easy for other people, and yet my life is in shambles, and I don't know how to put it back together again.

I am angry that no one knows how I feel, and believe me—they don't want to know! Then everyone would be miserable!

I am angry that I will never be the same person again. I am forever changed.

I am angry that I miss this person, relationship, or home this much. The pain is so great that is makes me angry every time I think of it.

I am angry that I am left with all of this debt.

I am angry with this person for leaving me to suffer in such heartache.

I am angry that people don't want to be with me because I am angry!

I am angry because I am sad and can't find my way anymore. . .

Some people never leave this stage either; they are just angry for the rest of their lives. If you find yourself in this stage, you need to decide to leave this stage. You must find courage and decide to confront the crucial next stage, the stage of "what if" and "if only."

Guilt and Depression—
The Torture of "What If" and "If Only"

Surely, it must be my fault. It is my fault. If only I had done or said or reacted or anticipated or noticed or called or hugged or prevented or, or, or. If only I had been a different person, then none of this would have happened. This is my punishment. I am guilty for this death (or end of relationship). If I had known that this person would die, then I would surely have been a better person in every conceivable way.

If I hadn't married him, then none of this would have happened. It must be my fault.

I feel so guilty that I have dug this really big dark hole, and now I have climbed into it and am staying there. No point coming out to enjoy life. Enjoy life? What is that anyway? All those pleasant, well-meaning people enjoying their perfect lives— Who do they think they are anyway? My life is miserable! I am completely alone!

If only I had not said those angry words before he left that day.

What if I had been driving instead of her? Would she still be alive today?

If only I hadn't been angry; perhaps I wouldn't have distracted him.

If I had taken the kids to school, I would have remembered the baby in the back seat. He was so distracted when he left that day.

If only I had kissed him goodbye that morning, maybe he would remember my love.

If only I had one more day, one more minute, surely I would be able to tell them how much I love them.

Guilt always seeks punishment, and then the depression follows. The path down this long dark road is a lonely one indeed. It is never necessary to travel this road, but a surprising number of people opt for a first-class ticket on this depressing guilt train. However, there is hope; no one has to stay on this train forever. The person must choose. Guilt and depression, anger and despair are needlessly hard on many a good heart. Remembering to love yourself is the first step to stopping this horrible guilt train.

Just because something terrible happened does not mean that you have to feel guilty, grief-stricken, or depressed for the rest of your life. That is a harsh choice. One of the surest ways to begin to climb out of the pit of despair is to think back to your actions. Most people are truly good people. When there is a death, you seem to forget your own goodness. You would be wise to think back to all the good things you did for that person or in that situation. If you look at past actions and choose not to have changed them if you had the chance, then you can release the "if only" concept. Sometimes it is just a person's time to leave this life or for a marriage or relationship to end. Sometimes there is no explanation for why something happens the way it does, and punishing yourself will never get you to a place of healing. Remembering your own goodness will help you to begin to move forward.

Some people also stop here and believe wrongly that they are to be punished forever. It is wiser to choose life instead of emotional death. If they do leave this stage, some enter the next one, which is feeling self-pity.

Jealousy, Anxiety, and "Poor Me"

Of all the emotions that we humans can experience, the two most powerful ones are love and fear. Jealousy and anxiety are subsets of fear. Hence, if you are jealous, there is then a fear that there is not enough for you. If you can understand that jealousy is fear with a grasping face, you can surely decide to change that aspect of yourself.

Look at all those cheerful people with their kids and spouses. They have what I used to have but don't anymore. Maybe I will never have this. I just don't want to hear about their kids or how their spouse is doing. I just don't want to hear how happy they are. They have what I can never have again—a great life. My life is ruined, RUINED! Why don't all those sickeningly sweet people just leave me alone? Do-gooders. Who do they think they are with all the answers—always trying to help me, to invite me? Why do they bother? Does it make them feel good trying to help me? What are they thinking? I know I will never be happy again.

Jealousy, anxiety, and the "poor-me" attitudes represent the fear that you will never be happy again. The tragedy is that you attract what you fear the most. This is also a drama that can either linger for years or occur not at all. Some who go through this stage actually may find themselves feeding on the drama of their pain and slowly but surely shutting out all their friends, family, co-workers, and anyone who can truly help them. You can become addicted to your own pain. Since pain has become your identity, you feed off the sympathy of others. This can either last the rest of your life or be extremely short-lived.

Fear can also consume you through the feeling of endless anxiety. You know that tragedy can happen at any time to anyone, and you have a terrible time conquering your fears. Sleep becomes a continual problem. Your body becomes extremely acidic with the continual squirts of adrenalin that feed this fear. The cycle has to be broken. The less sleep you have, the greater and greater become your levels of fear. The best way for you to heal this is to ask for outside help to conquer this fear. At this level, it is very difficult to do this alone; you must allow someone to help you.

This stage, however, does not have to happen. Many people never reach it because they understand that they are not punished; they do not feel guilt, and they are not afraid that there is not enough love for them. Love heals us. Jealousy makes us sick at heart. It is wonderful to know that there are such generous-of-heart people that, even in their grief, they can readily share the joy of others. This is what enables them to heal faster and reach the stage of acceptance sooner.

Acceptance

Acceptance for what has changed in your life is an amazing thing. It takes you to a new level. This path of change may take you through the long dark night of the soul. This path can either continue to keep you in darkness or lead you out of this darkness into a wonderful path of light—a place of tremendous growth for what you have become. Eventually, you may be able to see yourself in the following way:

I cannot change what has happened. It is now part of who I am. I am changed forever. I am different. This is not necessarily bad or good. It is just what is. I am still a good person. I am still loved. I am still able to love others and to be of service. I will always love the person who has left. I shall miss the spouse to whom I am no longer married. Even though this terrible storm took my home, I will have a new home and will always have fond memories of the old home I had.

I have changed. The world has changed. As I look around, I can see finally that everyone is going through something. The illusion that everyone but me is happy is just that—an illusion. Everyone is suffering from something. Everyone needs caring and compassion. As I have come to accept this reality, I am finding myself less de-

pressed and noticing more genuinely good days. I can be cheerful again. It is okay to stop grieving and to be happy again. I am me again, and not me. I am new because the old me had to go through this long dark night of the soul to be this new me. I am a good person. I love myself. I am really healing. I am all right.

When you can get to this level, you will have moved a very long way forward in your emotional and spiritual growth, which is ultimately the goal of experiencing this path of change. Even if a person stops here, this is a significant level of emotional and spiritual progress. Yet, there are people who do move forward to the next level of healing: forgiveness, compassion, and healing.

Forgiveness, Compassion, and Healing

This final stage actually takes you to a whole new level. This is the stage of soul evolution and soul maturity. This is the stage where you finally realize that all that has occurred to you has happened for your greater good, no matter how hard it may have been. There is no punishment—only learning and evolution.

This is the stage where you can readily forgive all the people who have caused you pain or left you. You are never abandoned or alone. When you can forgive them for physically leaving you, you will have achieved a tremendous level of understanding.

You can have compassion for what caused them to leave. You can accept that the karmic wheel continues to turn, no matter what. No one is immune. Having compassion for everyone opens your hearts to all that is and propels you to the next spiritual level of healing.

You heal when you have compassion for the people who left you and when you understand that they miss you, too.

You heal when you have compassion for all those involved in helping you through your pain, for it was their pain, too.

You heal when you forgive yourself for anything you may have said in your grief and pain. You heal when you can also forgive others for things they may have thoughtlessly said to you when they were raw with their own grief.

You heal when you can forgive any situation that is painful and know that it no longer has to be painful.

You heal when you accept that you will see your loved one again, that your divorce was after all for your greater good, and that the house you loved will be replaced with something that will further your learning on some level.

You heal when you finally accept that you were willing to do whatever it took to heal and to know joy again.

You heal when you see yourself performing service for others and feeling their love come to you in return.

You know that you are healed when your heart is light and full of love when you think of the loved one who is gone.

You are healed when you are grateful for this learning experience and forgive that which created it.

You are healed when you can simply love with abandon because your heart is so full of wonder at all that you have learned.

4

GRIEF TOOLS

The only constant in life is change.   Tina Erwin

Exploring Grief Tools

If you are grieving, you feel very alone. You can't imagine that anyone has ever felt this much pain; it's almost unbelievable. And yet, despite your pain, you still have to go on living, doing, and being. You still have to continue doing all the mundane things of life, from laundry to homework, bill paying to yard work. The ordinary still requires your attention. Everything has changed, and yet nothing has changed. You don't understand and cannot wrap your brain around the concept that everything you ever thought you knew about yourself, your plans for the future, and your whole life could change in one flash of a moment.

As hard as it is to realize, you do have to come to terms with your responsibilities as the one who is still living or having to deal with whatever is causing you to grieve. Perhaps friends and family members are looking to you for direction—what to do next or what not to do. They do not know how to comfort you. Your job will be to tell them.

You also have to learn how to go back to day–to–day living and yet still deal with the aftermath of whatever has caused this grief. This might range from making funeral arrangements to dealing with personal possessions or to returning to work and/or school. You will also have to deal with family dynamics, and that is often its own challenge.

The tools listed below may help with removing those helpless feelings during these times or enable you to help someone else with these feelings based on the various kinds of deaths or types of grief.

Crying Is a Natural Part of Grieving

In the process of grieving, it is important to understand that you may feel flooded by the emotion of all that is happening. Even if you work with a good grief counselor, you need to know that it is okay to cry. There is the school of thought that says you should tough it out and not cry over the grief feelings that you have. This is wrong. Crying is the natural way to express grief. Grief that is unexpressed literally backs up into the system and harms the body. At the least, sinus problems and watery eyes represent unprocessed grief, guilt, and unspent tears. At the most extreme form, unspent tears and profound sadness manifest in the body in the form of heart problems and/or heart attacks. Metaphorically, heart pain represents the person's emotionally sad heart. Very old grief seems to be stored in the kidneys. Perhaps if a person had been allowed to express his or her grief through the positive use of tears, he or she might have healed all of the organs of the body that were profoundly affected by grief.

Always remember that it is all right to cry. You can get to the other side of tears. Tears allow you to release the emotion in a healthy way for the body; this is why they were designed. In this process, you expend your energy with your salty, often painful crying. The salty sea is cleansing and so are tears. Once you are finished with this process, you will feel like a different person. Processing grief transmutes the energy of this powerful emotion, no matter when the grief happened. Releasing your tears represents compassion for yourself.

How to Help a Grieving Person or Family

Helping the family who has lost a loved one is very much like assisting a person who is dying. Perhaps part of the grieving person feels as if he or she is dying inside, and that person is going to need all the love and compassion, all the patience and kindness you can muster to help him or her through this time.

People in mourning need to be reminded that what they are feeling, in a weird sort of way, is normal. At this point in their lives, the shock of the death still weighs heavily upon them, and the concept of "normal" feelings seems out of place. However, if you are assisting someone, it is important for both of you to understand that these feelings are normal, healthy elements of the grieving process.

Remember, this is a time usually without precedent in their lives. Mostly, they have no frame of reference with which to understand the wave after wave of devastating feelings that hit them. Assisting them will tax you at every emotional level. It will tax you at the physical level, as well, because you will be tired as you go through this process with them. However, your service will be invaluable to them and can mean the difference between healing their grief with grace and wisdom or allowing it to remain unhealed for a very long time. Compassion helps no matter when you give it. Remember that you can also send love and prayer to a person who has died, no matter how long ago it happened.

When you first hear of the grief situation and you approach the family member, be aware that saying *"If you need anything, please call me, or let me know if I can help"* translates as *"I really don't know what to say, so I hope you won't call because I don't know how to help you deal with your grief."* Here are some suggestions of things to say when speaking to a grieving person or family, which do help with grief:

• *"I know that your loved one loved you very much."* (If you know this to be true). This may cause the person to cry, and this is healing because the salty tears are cleansing and remind the person of love, not loss.

• *"Her death was so sudden, and I know there are many things that you wish you could have said to her. Perhaps we can talk about it soon—I will call you—I know it helps to talk about it."* When you do get together, suggest that the grieving

person go ahead and tell the soul who has died anything he or she
wants to and share the feelings of the moment, allowing this opportunity for the voicing of any emotion.

- *"I want you to know that, although he is not physically here, you can still
communicate with him. As you go to sleep at night, tell him how you feel, now and
forever; it is okay to say that you miss him, because he misses you, too."*

- *"I sense that you feel lost without her; so as you drift off to sleep, ask for her
help. She loved you so much that, even though she is physically gone, she never
stopped loving you, and that love goes on for eternity and can still be communicated
to you."*

- (The loss of a child is really tough, no matter what the age.) *"We are
not privy to the reasons a child lives a brief life. I like to think that they were angels in
training and that they needed only a few more brief experiences before they moved on.
How special and how exquisitely hard to be one of those parents. This does not diminish your pain, I know, but perhaps you can feel that your child is truly special and
will always love you and be grateful for the sacrifice you made in loving him or her
so deeply and letting go so that perhaps your little one may be of help to others."*

- (The death of a parent creates serious feelings of abandonment. If
the parent dies and the person is young, the feelings are intensified.)
*"Although your mom or dad is gone, never forget that he or she will never, ever stop
loving you. As long as there are stars in the sky, your mom or dad will love you and
one day will be right there when it is your turn to go home. We don't always know
the reason that a person goes home early, but you must respect that reason and keep
on loving, not only your parent but yourself. Perhaps you were selected for this task
because you are so special. The death of your mom or dad is not a punishment for
you. You are offered many lessons; perhaps eternal love is one being offered to you
now."*

- *"You have always been a terrific son or daughter, and I know that your dad
was truly proud of you. I watched how hard you worked to do all the right things,
and I just know that he appreciated it and would tell you so if he were physically here.
But as you go to sleep at night, tell him your thoughts, and you may be able to hear his
answer; for, although he has physically left, he did not spiritually leave, and he never
will."*

- If you do not know what to say, if the moment is so powerful, it is
acceptable just to hug that person with all your heart. Hug the person
often and understand that when a person is grieving, he or she will

need more physical contact—not less. Rub this person's hand or back. Hold his or her hand. *Be there for this person.*

• If many months have passed and you are with your grieving friend, and he or she seems fine when all of a sudden an emotion wells up and there are tears, do not feel embarrassed about it. Say *"It is okay to cry. Just let the tears come."* Hold him or her. Ask what caused the tears and let the person talk about it. This is what it means to really be there for someone.

• What if you feel like crying with the person? This is just fine. It is comforting for that person to know that you are moved to tears, as well. He or she will not feel so alone, and a special kinship will be formed. Tears are really wonderful for helping us cleanse our souls of powerful emotions.

Also, keep in mind that grieving is really hard work. It is hard for the person grieving, and it is hard if you are the one helping with someone's grief. This is really compassion in action. This is also a precious time for you to do tremendous service. When you are tired or feel your patience ebbing, just remember that this is really the compassion you will want for yourself.

Releasing Attachment: The Transmuting Process

Why is there physical pain with grief or sometimes vomiting and shock when someone dies? This is due to the fact that you connect to people, animals, places, and things, and you literally create subtle attachments. You even use the word, saying how "attached" you were to the person, place, or thing.

One of the elements that helps you to heal is the understanding that you have attachments to everything. Eventually you have to learn how to cut, sever, release, and transmute those attachments to people, places, and things.

Sometimes people feel that grief is so painful that they may wonder if it wouldn't be better not to love at all in order to shield themselves from the attachments that relationships with anyone or any creature bring. Your path to enlightenment is predicated on your ability to learn about all the facets of love. You must learn through living and dying all the ways in which you can love and be loved. One way of understanding love is through the concept of the polarity that is death. After a death, you never look at things quite the same way again Death offers you the opportunity to appreciate life, relationships, and even things in a totally new and perhaps more grateful way. Such is the polarity of death.

It is important that you also understand how profound these attachments are on other levels. The Hawaiian Huna tradition believes that these physical attachments are real. They considered them to be a unique form of energy even though you cannot see them with your physical eyes. Rather like electricity, which you cannot see but know exists, this type of energy comes from your own life force. In the Huna tradition, these attachments are called *aka cords*. These aka cords emanate out from your solar plexus—the area just below your breastbone. This is the place where the cord extends out and makes attachments to everyone you have ever met, to every place you have ever been, and to everything you have ever owned. The longer you are attached or connected to something, someone, or someplace, the stronger your aka cord is. Your thoughts also flow along these fine, filament–like energetic cords. This is why when you are connected to someone and that person is thinking about you, you often sense it. This is also why if you have powerful cords attached in a strong love relationship, you often feel it immediately when the person dies. There are many ways to understand how these cords are eventually cut. The more profound the relationship, the thicker are the aka cords of attachment.

When a person dies a long, lingering death, or even an expected death, friends and family members begin cutting these attachments. In this situation, cutting a cord means to begin to imagine the person out of pain and in a better place. So, when the person does die, the cord has become so thin that grief work is not as profound. Friends and family have already begun to transmute their connection to that person. You are well on the road to healing your grief.

However, if the death is sudden, completely unexpected, tragic, or horrific, these emotional cords are instantly cut. As the person's life force leaves, your connecting aka cords come recoiling back to you. Since these cords flow from your solar plexus, you feel sick at your stomach. If the loss is a family member, your cords are amazingly thick, because there is or was total love for that person. The loss makes you sick because the cords are cut so quickly that there is no time to transmute the energy that connected you to that person.

This is why, for example, a person who has lost a child feels as though part of him or her dies, because the cord goes to the root of the parent. Healing can take place if the parent can transmute this pain by working through all the stages of grief.

Grief for an animal is especially painful, because animals give us unconditional love. Our aka cords are very strongly attached to them. This is also why when we hear animal cruelty stories, we almost universally feel bad. We cannot bear to hear of mistreatment of an animal because we have such strong attachments to the animal kingdom.

You are also deeply attached to places and things. The "Old Homestead" or the house where you grew up—imagine the attachments there! You would have touched everything! When it is sold to someone else, you have a period of grief. This applies to a piece of art, a favorite mug, a sweater, any physical object, or a relationship. When it breaks, you have grief—momentarily, probably—but you grieve. You grieve more if a special person gave it to you, because there are dual cords attached to the object. Places elicit emotion, as well, since you have attachments there, too, some stronger than others. If a place were negative, you unconsciously made sure that you did not attach a very strong cord. This is because you would not have loving memories of such an awful place. If you were attached to a great place, there would be lots of cords attached there. That is why if there is a natural disaster, you find yourself saying, "I was there," or "I stood right in that spot!" You have a certain degree of grief because you left a cord attached.

What if you didn't know you had a connection to a place or a thing or a group of people? Sometimes you grieve for things that occurred in past lives but are not aware of it. Perhaps the best example is the movie *Titanic*. Why did people see it four and five times? Perhaps it was because in some way or another they did have a connection to another place and time with similar circumstances where they were not permitted to grieve.

Hopefully, by realizing that you do have these attachments to so many people, places, and things, you can begin to understand on a greater level the process of detaching from them.

Detached Compassion

What is detached compassion? It is the concept that you can have compassion for someone without becoming completely involved in the drama of the situation. This enables you to have a much better perspective on the entire aspect of learning and growing. Your service to the person, family, or situation can be much greater because your own emotions are not tangled up in their need for help. This can be critically essential in a grief situation. If you are going to help, you have to find it within yourself to be detached from some of the most heart-wrenching aspects of the sadness. If you are able to do this, you may find that you can do it only for short periods of time. Grieving is just hard work. Helping someone else grieve is exceptionally challenging. It is harder if you cannot find it within yourself to detach from some level of the pain.

There is another aspect to detached compassion. Often in a grief situation, the person may want to stay within the pain and drama of the event for an extended period of time. The person may not welcome any of your attempts to help him or her heal. It is important to keep in mind that wanting to help is terrific, but if the person wants to experience the entire event without your help, that is the person's choice, and your job is to respect this choice. Be compassionate, and then move on. You cannot want something for someone that he or she does not already want. You have to let go. In a sense this frees you from the feeling of responsibility that comes from the need to help someone or to work on a situation in which you can do nothing else to make a difference. Know what you can and cannot do. Do only that, and then detach.

Detached compassion will enhance your overall service mission and make your service more powerful in the long run. You cannot heal everyone. Not everyone wants to be healed. Again, your job is to help where you can and then to move on.

The Power of Focused Prayer

How does prayer help a grieving family? It is important to understand that a person's faith is irrelevant when it comes to prayer, for the power of prayer, the intention of prayer, is intrinsic to the person sending it. If that person has positive love in his or her heart, then the object of the prayer will receive that positive energy. By being aware of the physics behind why your prayers can help, you can send these prayers more deliberately and can also understand why the recipients are all so grateful.

How, for example, in the instance of a child's death, does the family feel prayer? What is it like? When a child dies, it is as if you cannot breathe; you cannot wrap your brain around the reality of the chilling moment of finality. It is in these critical moments that prayer comes to you as a form of energy—it literally lifts you up. Prayer enters your aching body as little bright spots of hope and light that take seed in the recesses of your aching heart. Prayer helps you manage the pain and then heal the pain. It takes time and energy, the energy of others, to help anyone in this situation.

Many people send angels to help. Some ask that healing be given to the aching hearts of the family, and some wrap the family in the energy of their (the senders') love. Prayer is felt, even in the meltdown moments, and those moments do not last as long or perhaps are not quite as severe. Sometimes the presence of the angels is felt, especially at the funeral. Many times family members are able to laugh out loud at the funny and memorable things that the departed person was famous for, and the family's laughter and memories are treasured.

One astounding aspect is that prayers sent to grieving family members enable them to think more clearly about what they have to do in each moment and the decisions that have to be made. If family members can often receive this subtle energy of prayer, they can be more aware and able to function in the early days following a death.

Prayers help the grieving family enter a different phase, one of acceptance and learning how to live—not survive—but live as whole people without the charming personality of the one who is no longer physically in their lives. They know that he or she is in the heaven world and is actively participating in soul evolution. The family can use prayer differently now to help with the irritability and, eventually, to empower acceptance.

Prayer is the fuel of the universe itself. It is the energy of love, and it helps to heal the sender and the recipient.

5

HEALING GRIEF

Then we say, when our loved ones, our heart's desires are taken from us, in what are we to believe?
Edgar Cayce Reading 1567-2

Why Is Healing Grief Difficult?

Grief is the process of healing yourself and of understanding the new person you are becoming as a result of this event. You can either choose to stay in a place of depression and despair for what can never be the same or you can take that same set of circumstances and use them to create a better person, making all those around you better for the experience. You choose your pain, and you choose your healing. Grief can be healed. So the task before you is to understand what helps your healing and what things complicate or impede it.

If death is a process of re-creation, then why aren't you happy for a person when he or she returns for this re-creation process? Why do you feel relief, shock, physical pain, nausea, numbness, lament, anguish, torture, guilt, anger, and rage? Why are you seldom ready for death when it comes, whether it's your own or a loved one's? It is because you have been taught to fear death as something horrible like the Grim Reaper or like someone who will "smite" you with a mighty sword. Death is vengeance for some, disaster and complete tragedy for others. Often, it is the cold price of peace or the tragic price of war. Death is power to some, relief to a few, and an escape for others. It doesn't matter how you view it; you still feel some sense of grief when a death occurs. How you respond to grief may have quite a bit to do with the method of a person's death.

The Method of Death Determines the Path of Healing

The speed with which friends and family can heal is in direct proportion to the method by which an individual dies. While other factors are always operative, this particular aspect has a profound effect on the people who are left to grieve. The following examples illustrate this concept.

If a person is 100 years old and dies a peaceful death in sleep, all parties will grieve. However, the grief will generally not be severe, will not last for a long time, and can be gracefully brief. The reasons are that there was no trauma to the person's body and that there was no further expectation for that soul in this lifetime. This scenario has a sense of logical completion and grace.

If a person has a long, lingering illness, emotional healing after death is faster because of the understanding that the person is no longer in pain. You miss the person, but you would not wish to prolong the suffering he or she was experiencing. That would be selfish; you can work through this feeling. Your grief will center more on the life the person did not get to live. This is where the concepts of reincarnation can be helpful. Perhaps in the next life the person will get to have a longer life.

If a person is a soldier or a peace officer and dies in the line of duty, you can heal this grief by acknowledging that the person knew the risks and this was his or her life choice done in the service of humanity. When a person dies in the line of service, there is nobility to this person's death, and those left behind remember how much the person loved his or her fellow human beings, and you can be proud of who he or she was. This view can mitigate, to a certain degree, the pain of the person's loss.

Death by an accident of any kind is traumatic because of the suddenness of the event. Healing this grief will depend largely on the type of accident and the damage to the person's body. The shock of the event may eventually give way to understanding that some people do not come to live a long life. Some souls come to mortal life for only a limited time, and when that time is over, they leave. There has to be a method for their departure, and frequently, that is by some type of accident. Understanding this concept of a limited life span may help in healing this type of grief. Sometimes you have to honor the life path of another.

Contrast this situation with the death of a child by any means. The trauma for the family of a child who has died can be severe, and that severity is further exacerbated by the method of the child's death. In our minds, children aren't supposed to die, and parents aren't supposed to outlive their children. You have an expectation for them, for their lives, and for your life with them. If their method of death, however, is peaceful and if they die in their sleep or of a sudden infection, then you can begin to accept the facts that perhaps it was their time to go and perhaps they were meant to be here for only a short time. In a parent's bewilderment, there can be some comforting logic.

However, if a child is murdered and if that child's body is then further mutilated or damaged, then it is extremely difficult for the family to understand, to accept, to forgive, and to ever find peace. There is a sense of unfathomable outrage and pain that takes a very long time to heal.

The murder of a person of any age creates tremendous additional trauma for families and friends left behind. Families of murder victims have a very hard time healing their grief and ever feeling normal again. The incidence of violence in their lives acts like a hideous contaminant that they cannot seem to cleanse. They will need special help, care, and focused effort to heal. Their path to wholeness and forgiveness will be considerably longer. Family members are not going to be able to just "get over it."

If a friend or family member commits suicide, this method of death can be extremely traumatic not only because of the specific death method but also because of the attendant social stigma. Relatives of a suicide frequently assume that they will be judged as having somehow failed the person who died. There is a subtle level of implied guilt. These people will require a special level of love and compassion to heal this grief.

If you are to understand how to help yourself or someone else who is grieving, you must understand that the dynamics of the method of death are a crucial element in a person's healing. No matter what the circumstances of a death, healing is possible. It just takes time, insight, hope, a great deal of prayer, and a genuine desire to work on forgiving themselves and the person who has died.

Removing the Helpless Feelings During Grief

There is helplessness in grief, a feeling that there is nothing more that can be done for the person who has died or for a situation that has happened. This is not so. There is a tremendous amount that can be done to help a soul. There is also much that can be done to heal relationships after a death and to help those who are suffering the grief.

Prayers always benefit the soul everyone is grieving. Prayers help the soul no matter how long ago the person died. Whatever the method of death, prayers are a source of loving energy for the soul, who is always grateful for them.

Consider doing things that will honor the memory of the soul. This can be as simple as planting a tree or garden in the person's honor. When you are ready, make a donation to a foundation seeking a cure for whatever took this person's life, or donate the person's clothes or other belongings to a charity.

Talk about the person who has died. Do it every day. Don't be afraid to refer to that person or talk about things he or she did. There is often a fear that precious memories will be lost. Talking about the person keeps these memories alive.

If the person was extremely giving, there will be a really tremendous sense of loss: What will all of us do without him or her? Decide to be more like this person and try to adopt the positive qualities this person held. Emulating the person will be a fitting testimony to his or her life.

If the person was difficult and/or cruel, you may not feel helpless, but you may feel an odd sense of release and relief. Find someone you can trust and share your feelings honestly. Telling the truth about how you feel can be most beneficial.

Contacting neighbors, friends, and family members and talking to them about your days will help healing.

Sending prayer to the person who has left will also help you to heal because you are doing something positive. Following the steps to enjoying this person's memory will enable healing to continue.

Reconnecting to the divine in any way you can will greatly expand your heart and open you up to the healing energies of the heavens. Faith heals and prayer heals. The combination of the two is critical to believing that you can heal.

Realize that you are never going to be the same. All experiences change you, and these changes can make you stronger, more compassionate, or bitter. You can continue to feel helpless or decide to be productive. You must choose. This person's death is an opportunity either to grow or to stay frozen at the moment of this event. You are always given the opportunity to decide how your life will proceed from this moment on.

Physical Healing After a Death

When someone you love dies, or when a relationship ends, your body goes through physical changes. If the death is extremely sudden, you are flooded with adrenaline, which makes your body extremely acidic. A large rush of adrenaline can make anyone nauseated, lightheaded, or physically sick. You often do not feel you can even think straight. However, there are gentle remedies that can dramatically help you or any grieving person to return to an alkaline level and to accelerate the process of healing. If you feel that your friend or family member is open to this, suggest any or all of the remedies described in this section or make a gift basket that includes them.

How do you know if you are not healing? Your body will tell you. You may find that you experience chronic sinus problems, such as headaches, infections, colds, and flu. Often kidney and colon problems are symptoms of old grief. Recent grief lives in the sinuses. Sadness lives in the heart. If you find that you have problems in these areas, you may not have dealt fully with new and old grief.

Here are some specific immediate and long-term grief remedies that may return a thoroughly acidic body back to an alkaline state.

• Homeopathic remedies: *Lycopodium, Arnica Montana,* or *Ignatia Imara* by Boiron.

• Cell salts: These work to return the chemical nature of the cell to normal. Specifically, try Bioplasma by Hylands. Follow package directions.

• Bach Flower Remedies: Rescue Remedy, Rescue Sleep, Star of Bethlehem, Sweet Chestnut, Walnut, and Agrimony. Take three times a day. These remedies are very gentle and work subtly on the body. It is a quiet change that allows the body to heal in a very simple way.

• Essential oils: lavender, frankincense, sweet orange oil, and many others assist a person with the grieving process and provide much gentle relief. Use lavender and frankincense in a base of castor oil on feet to help restore balance. This is an especially wonderful combination to use on the feet of children who are grieving. Use sweet orange oil in a spray mister in bedrooms or anywhere someone has been grieving. It shifts the energy and makes things feel cleaner.

• Noni Juice from the *Morinda Citrifolia* plant and Mangosteen juice are antioxidant juices and blood cleansers, which quickly speed the body back to an alkaline balance. Four to eight ounces a day spread throughout the day are suggested for someone experiencing severe grief. These remedies also help depression. Even pomegranate and grape juice are beneficial for the body.

• Holy Basil is an herb that specifically helps keep a person's mood more upbeat by balancing body chemistry.

• Probiotics help the body to process food and helps to keep bodies healthy.

• Acupuncture is a great tool to open blocked areas of the body. Be sure to ask specifically for grief assistance for the body.

• Therapeutic massage helps relax the tense muscles and eases out emotional pain.

• Salt baths: place 2–4 pounds of sea salt, Epsom, or Kosher salt in very warm bath water. Add essential oil of lavender to the water. Soak in this salty lavender–filled water for at least thirty minutes and then rinse. Complete this bathing regimen 3 times a week to cleanse the body of dark and depressing feelings.

• Vitamins: B–complex, timed–release vitamin C, E, and calcium along with other essential minerals restore the chemical balance of the body. There are a host of other vitamins that help the body. This must be a conscious personal and financial commitment. If you feel physically better, you can face grief with more courage. Be sure to take these vitamins with food.

• Water: Drink lots of pure water with a lemon wedge. The lemon turns the acid aspect of the water to alkaline and helps bring balance to the body.

• Music: Playing gorgeous music by Mozart, Vivaldi, New Age artists, Charlotte Church, Sarah Brightman, or Sissel lifts you up and inspires you. Even if the music makes you cry, you are releasing the feelings and are on the road to healing.

The most essential point is that there is not just one thing that will help this process. It is a combination of things—a layered approach that begins to touch and to heal *all* the parts of you—that makes a difference. Even if you may not feel like doing all of these things, the act of doing even some of them will accelerate your healing.

Things That Retard Healing and Are to Be Avoided

Death is a time of great shock. It is not unusual to reach for over–the-counter aids and various other remedies to help yourself. However, some of them will make your body feel terrible and will significantly retard healing.

• Antidepressants: These treat only the symptoms of grief but never address the deep pain.

• Sleep aids: With grief comes the vicious cycle of fatigue. Avoid sleep aids after the first period of shock. Taking something to fall asleep is not unusual in the early days of grief, but permanent insomnia may be a symptom of not wanting to face the deeper meaning of all that has happened to you.

• Alcohol: Any type of this substance will create much greater levels of depression and must be avoided completely.

- Caffeine: Caffeinated drinks are also acid based and may add to sleeplessness, nervousness, depression, and anxiety. Avoid coffee and sodas.
- Drugs: These substances affect the body and react differently in a very acidic body or a body that has experienced shock. Be extremely careful about taking any kind of drug not absolutely necessary during this time. Drugs affect judgment, and during this time, you need the best judgment of your whole life.
- Tobacco: These products will also add to the acidic base of a person's body. If at all possible, avoid smoking.
- Fear–based television shows: News shows or any others that trivialize death will add to pain and anxiety. Avoid these shows.
- Noise: You will need peace and quiet. There is a physically fragile feeling after any traumatic death. Now is the time to be most kind to your body.

What Not to Say to Someone Who is Grieving

When someone is going through a grief situation, there are just some things that a person should not say because of the negative impact they will have on the grieving person.
- If someone loses a child, some of the worst things you can say are:
  "Well, at least you have other children."
  "You can have more children to replace the one who died."
  "You can always adopt; there are lots of kids who need families."
- If someone is dying of any disease, cancer, organ failure, whatever it is, do not say or do any of the following things:
  Chat about all the other people you know or knew who died of cancer.
  Talk about the person in the third person and as if he or she were already dead while you are in his or her presence.
  Talk about how other people worked until their last day and never gave in to the physical pain or how much better they looked at the end stages.
- If someone's spouse dies, do not say these things [which have been said at funerals]:
  "Well, look how young you are, you can always remarry. Would you like me to

set you up?"
"You know he or she would want you to remarry."
"When you remarry, will you keep his or her things in the house?"
"Did he leave you anything? Was there insurance money? Was he or she a good spouse?"

- If there was a tragic accident, do not say these things:
  "How could you let this happen?"
  "Why wasn't someone watching them?"
  "How will you be able to live with yourself after this accident?"

The point here is that whenever you are in a situation where you are speaking to a grieving person always strive to be exceedingly circumspect in what you say. Edit what you say for the highest good. If you wonder whether you should say it, don't. Sometimes there are no words. Sometimes you just have to hold someone. Words said that hurt resound in the grieving person's head for a very long time. Be aware of this and always exercise your best judgment for the highest good of each situation.

What Really Helps Those Who Are Grieving?

People often talk about a sense of helplessness after a death of any kind. However, in truth, there are many things that can be done which will promote healing on all levels. While some things may seem more difficult than other things, all of them will help the healing process. The following sections are for all of those who are helping themselves or others through the process of healing grief.

Immediate Helpful Aids

People who feel compassion for a grieving family want to do something to help, yet they often do not know what to do. They often bring food and flowers. However, sometimes these things can be problematic. After a death, especially a sudden death, people do not feel like eating because their bodies are full of adrenalin. Hence when friends and neighbors bring food to a family that has experienced a death sometimes there is so much food that the grieving family does not feel like eating the wonderful donations and does not have room to refrigerate the generous offerings.

Sometimes a better approach would be to bring paper goods that can be disposed of easily so dishes don't have to be done, and quick fix items for breakfast that do not require refrigeration. However, if you do bring food, be sure to put your name on the serving dish.

The best gift is actually either a gift basket that includes things that do not have to be chilled or a gift card to a restaurant, grocery store/ deli, a coffee house, or a movie theater or even just cash, so that the family can have an evening out. Grieving people just don't feel like eating, and when they do, they won't cook. Also, movie tickets are helpful because sometimes you just have to have a break from the intensity of those powerful grieving moments. These ideas are especially helpful if there are children at home.

Many people send either living plants or bouquets of flowers. Living plants require care and are not always a good idea for a family that can barely get through each day. Fresh flowers mean a great deal to some families and others greatly dislike them and dispose of them immediately. If it is possible to inquire whether a family would like flowers, then this can be quite helpful.

Prayer Work for the Transitioned Soul

You can say specific prayers for the person who has transitioned to the heaven world. Say them for at least two months. The prayers in the Addendum were created to help the soul have an easier journey when entering the heaven world. Remember when you pray, you are closer to God. In those moments of heartfelt prayer, consider also asking for healing for everyone who is grieving anything. The more healing you can send out, the sooner will you feel your own heart begin to recover.

Diary of Intimate Letters to Your Loved One

Create a diary of letters written to the soul who has transitioned. This is your opportunity to tell this soul how you feel now, how you felt during his or her long or short life, and how much you miss this person.

You can even write your angry thoughts over the fact that he or she has left. Then, as a companion aspect, record how tenderly you forgive him or her for leaving. Eventually, this forgiveness for leaving you will be the ultimate aspect of healing for both parties. This will be a compassionate act for you and for the departed one, as well. Over time, as you read back over these letters, you will realize how you have grown and healed. Then the day will come when you no longer need to write these letters because you will have said everything that you felt needed to be said.

Treasure Box of Memories

Buy or create a beautiful treasure box that will hold 5" x 7" note cards. Each time a memory comes up of the person who has died, write it down. Ask friends and family to write down funny moments they remember, as well. These cards can be organized by age or topic as you wish. Some people are such wonderful characters that there are a million stories about them, and reviewing these episodes will help you heal. This activity is especially important if a parent or grandparent dies and young children may not remember the person. This is uniquely special if a child dies and you want to treasure every single precious moment you had. When all is said and done, at the end of a day and at the end of a life, all you ever really have are the memories of life's special moments and how you lived them.

Miracle Log Book

Many souls offer miracles to family and friends after their departure. Have a miracle log book ready to record those special moments. This keeps the person alive in your mind, heart, and memory. This helps you to understand that, although they may not be physically here with you, they have not stopped loving you. Many souls find unique and clever ways of letting you know this fact. Examples include finding pennies in front of you when you are thinking of the person. Some people actually sense the person's presence or smell the individual's aftershave or fragrance. Chart synchronicities that have happened since this person left.

You helped someone in the person's name, you asked the person for help, and an answer was given to you. There are many magical, wonderful moments that can occur after a death if you can just look for them, and if you can look forward to their coming your way because you are open to the miracles that can be found around you.

Memory Gathering

Invite all of your loved one's friends over for a memory gathering. Let them know how you are doing. Ask them to bring a memory of your family member with them, either written or not. Then laugh about all the wonderful things this soul meant to you; enjoy his or her personality. Death is not an end; it is only a transition from one realm to another, and your laughter will enable everyone to feel better about his or her grief as well as your own. Even if you cry, it is still okay because the salt of tears is ultimately healing. Your openness will go a long way in helping others to heal. Many people refuse to ever talk about a person after he or she has died; this is not healing. Your memories of the loved one are going to persist for a very long time. It is always healing to open your heart to remembering the person.

Honoring the Person

If your grief is because of a physical death, create something that honors the person. This can be anything as simple as a rose garden or a piece of artwork to something as sophisticated as a foundation or scholarship fund in the person's name. Give to a library or service agency in his or her name. Honoring the person helps not just you but also the soul. This type of honoring means that you valued him or her and that this value continues on long after the anniversary of the person's death.

Learning from a Difficult Person

If the person you are grieving was a profoundly difficult person and if this person emotionally or physically harmed you, it is even more important to work through grief on a practical level. If you are glad he or she is gone, then do not hesitate to write these things down. Part of your healing is acknowledging what happened between you two in that challenging relationship. This is an extremely important time to decide to learn from this person. If this person did not love you, then you would have learned the importance of love. If the person abused you, then your lesson would be the value of kindness, compassion, and caring. If this person created guilt feelings in you, then you can know the power of releasing this guilt and of learning to be your own person. Difficult people are placed in your life to teach you precious, often hard-won lessons. You can use grief to heal parts of your life that may have been hurt by this person. Sometimes, the most difficult person is your greatest teacher if you can bring yourself to see it that way.

The Concepts of Faith and Healing: There Is No Healing Without God

There is so much to do after a death or trauma that, at first, the concept of healing is a low priority. You have to deal with the shock of the immediate concerns: the cause of death, the disposition of the body, the funeral, flowers, the visitors, and the cards. You wonder what to say to people, and whether or not the house is clean enough. You try to resist the urge to vomit all of the time, and your nights are plagued by the inability to sleep. You wonder how there can be all these people around, and yet you feel separate from them. They go home to their families, and your family will never be the same again.

Perhaps the first step is to ask for help not just from a family member or neighbor but by remembering your connection to God. There is no healing without God. Ask for help. Ask for angels of compassion for you and other grieving friends and family members. It is often hard to remember to do this, but if you can, this request will lift the darkness and continue to do so for quite awhile. It is important to remember that you are not being punished, although you may think this is the case as you experience the most severe emotional pain of your entire life. God does not abandon us in our darkest moments. The faith, love, and compassion of God are there if you can open yourself up to these wonderful feelings. This will also help when you begin to receive the answers to the nagging question of why this happened.

Changing Course after a Person Has Died

When you have a relationship with someone, you have a momentum that goes along with that relationship. You have spent time learning all about this person. You have developed a comfort zone with him or her. You have built-in expectations at an extremely mundane level. The person goes to work and comes home. You eat supper together. You go to bed together. You are planning what to do this weekend or next week. You plan, live, and hope together. You do things together. There is a balance that exists between and among people that brings you comfort. You have an unconscious expectation that this person in your life will be there tomorrow. It makes you feel safe and secure.

You have a momentum of unspoken expectations with that person. You have charted a course with him or her, no matter who the person is to you. This momentum is like a supertanker going at high speed, following a charted course, and suddenly having its engines shut down. The tanker shudders. The engines stop—but the momentum continues. It takes many miles to stop a supertanker—the built-up momentum is that great—and it takes a very long time for the momentum of a relationship to come to a complete halt.

You have to figure out at which level the relation "ship" exists. You have to examine the course charted with that person, and you have to bring it to a halt. Then, you have to plan a new course, and you need to realize that you can chart it without that person by your side or in your life. No one can decide this but you.

Where are you going? What course do you chart? What will life be like now without this person? Do you have the courage to face this alone? Are you really alone? Who can help you? Can you ask for help? Do you have to go back to high speed, or can you move ahead slowly?

The answers to these questions lie within you and can be accessed by beginning to return to your faith in God and in yourself. When charting this new course, you have to ask for help and to look for the answers when they come. The tired cliché "when one door closes, another opens" is always true. You just have to be willing to see the opportunities as they come toward you. Sometimes you have to be still for awhile to see and to hear what is going to be the best for you. You have to be patient with yourself.

You have to accept that there is a new path and that it can be exciting. You had your own life before this person entered yours. Even if this person was a parent, you had a life in the heaven world before being born. You lived without him or her before, and you can do it again. You need to consider how you can do this and to work a little bit on it each day. If you are focused on understanding that you do have a new course to follow, you may find that your ability to chart this new course becomes easier as each new day unfolds.

Getting Back to Normal

Fatigue seems to be a constant companion, yet, no matter how tired you are, there are things to do. The mundane day-to-day tasks of laundry, shopping, cooking, putting gas in our car, answering the mail, and being the person you have always been continue: These things still need to be done. So, how do you start being that person again?

Steps to Returning to a Normal Routine

1. Make a list of what you want to do each day, but put only three things on this list. Consider that paying your bills is a top priority after a death, a divorce, or natural catastrophe. Many people have lost their credit rating because they were so depressed that they neglected to pay their bills for several months. If you complete one of those items on your list, you have had a successful day. Try this approach from thirty to forty-five days after the death.

2. Now increase the list to five things a day. If you get three or four of these done each day, you have a measure of progress.

3. On each list, each day, include resting and taking a nap. Rest is the surest way to healing because it empowers you to think more clearly. Grieving is just exhausting, so don't feel that it is wrong to rest. It is extremely important to maintain your personal health, and rest is the best way to stay healthy.

4. As soon as you possibly can, return phone calls and answer essential mail. Let other correspondences slide for up to a month; then take hold of your life and begin to answer all correspondences.

5. As soon as you can, start leaving your house. Go shopping; be with people. The more isolated you make yourself, the more isolated you will become and the slower you will heal. While it will seem hard at first, it is essential that you begin to experience the person you still are.

The Process of Disposition of Possessions

What do you do with a person's things after he or she dies or leaves? Mostly, you do nothing at first. Some people cannot even go into the room the person used to occupy. There are drawers and closets of clothes and toys. They smell like the person who isn't there. It seems like the last contact you have with the person is this scent—the fragrance, distinctive and precious. Touching these things reduces you to tears. It is all right to cry. It is all right to begin to let go of a box of this or that, slowly, in your own time. However, holding on forever is an emotional trap and one that will not serve you in the long run. You need to begin to give yourself small things to do that you are comfortable doing. For instance, if it is a child, go through the clothes he or she outgrew. You can give those to needy children first and see how you feel about this. An aspect of going through the loved one's room and clothes is the process of beginning to release the grasping part of your heart—that part of you that wants to hold on forever. Your subconscious is stubborn. It does not want to let go. You have to let go; it is this letting go that will heal you in the long run.

So how do you ever part with something that belonged to the person?

The answer is to consider the person and what he or she would want to happen to the clothes, toys, or tools. You should give yourself time to rest and to recover from the initial shock of the event and then begin this task. Do it slowly at first, as it may be quite painful. However, working through this process is an essential element of working through grief. Try these steps because they may help to bring some order after the chaos of dealing with a death:

1. Get out a box and fill it with clothing the person hated. Put those items in the box. This is not quite as hard as handling loved items. Do only this on the first day.

2. Next go to clothing the person never, ever wore—clothing that was old—or items you were trying to get them to let go of. Put these in the box.

3. Next work on clothing that has little sentimental value: They wore it, but when you hold it, it does not tug at you quite as much. Be honest. Not all clothing tugs at you.

4. Get out a new box. Now look at the clothing that the person loved. These are the pieces that really tug at your heart. Put all of this clothing in the box and label it "Favorite Clothing." Put this box away for safekeeping. Do not put in every piece of clothing the person owned. Pick just a few pieces. This creates balance and enables you to be selective in what you will ultimately keep.

5. Get out a new box. Get out the person's laundry and put this in this box. Label it "Last Laundry." This is often among the hardest things to do because these pieces of clothing smell like the person, and these pieces are often the hardest to part with, even to wash, because washing them is an act of accepting the transition. Put the date on it when you think you can finally wash them. You may change this date many times, or you may go through with the date. By assigning a date, you are telling yourself that you are in a process of healing and that by that date you will evaluate your level of healing.

Returning to Work

When to return to work or to school is a difficult question to answer. The feeling that you cannot bear talking to people may last for awhile, but people want you back right away. You feel that you are grieving as fast as you can. What is the answer?

Tell your employer, employees, and coworkers that you are returning, but that you may not be quite at 100%. Ask openly for their patience and assistance. If you are a grieving person, you will probably be very distracted, and your productivity may not be at its previous level.

Understand this about yourself. You may want to ask for a week of half days. This schedule may provide an easier transition for you. You may find that even working half days is exhausting and that you spend the other half of the day sleeping. This is okay. You have just experienced a severe life crisis, a massive trauma. This will require patience to heal.

If you find that you are crying constantly at work, you may have to seek a really good grief counselor. Remember, the inability to come to terms with grief is seldom about the person who transitioned. It is all about the grieving person's sense of emotional abandonment and rage or sadness. The answer is about healing yourself. It is about ceasing the concept of "look what happened to me" and changing it to compassion for the person who has left.

Changing Your Life

Life has changed. Realize that it has changed and that you are now changed. You will not be the same because of this event. This is simply the way it is. However, the new and changed you does not have to be permanently depressed, guilty, or empty. Part of the reason for this event, this death, or transition is that it is ultimately an opportunity for you to be different in a positive way. You are now faced with serious life choices. You can be sad, bitter, sullen, or victimized forever, or you can be grateful for the opportunity to chart a different course in your life. Giving yourself time to do this is important, but do not take forever. Set some dates; this will give you perspective on the changes you are encountering and help you organize your days in the aftermath of the chaos of grief.

Holidays

What do you do with holidays? How should you handle them? If someone dies at a religious holiday such as Christmas or Hanukah, do you ever celebrate this time again? What about birthdays? It is important to understand that times of celebration without this person are not going to be the same. You and your family will have to choose how you are going to manage these events. Perhaps you can sit down as a family and discuss it because holidays can become tortuous times of questionable celebration if you allow that to happen. Some families choose not to celebrate any occasion for a very long time, because they fear the emotion the occasion will engender. Other families decide to have a wonderful time and remember their beloved in their hearts in a positive way. Whatever choice you make will affect not just you personally, but your immediate family, friends and neighbors. It is wise to consider that very probably the person who has gone would not want anyone to stop living and celebrating life, certainly not on his or her account.

Perhaps there is a middle ground. If being merry will not be comfortable for you and your family for the first year or so following the death or divorce, then create a modified celebration. Have only a few decorations or a simple birthday cake without a gathering of people. In the coming years, anticipate returning to family celebrations, and make a toast to the family member who is not there. Acknowledging the person who is gone will relieve some subtle tension and empower your healing.

Life still goes on, so eventually you will want to continue to celebrate holidays and have a great time. Remember when your loved one was there and smile. Do not make holidays a dreaded event, or you will spoil them for everyone. Birthdays or anniversaries of the person are times to be celebrated—not grieved. You had those happy times together; remember them, love them, and then move forward.

What do you do about holiday cards? In the future, if you are not comfortable omitting the person's name, just sign it "Love, the Smith family," for example. Also, relate your situation in the card. Sometimes a straightforward explanation of what happened, how you are doing and that you are looking forward to continuing your relationship with your friend or friends can be a wonderful tool in your healing process.

The Anniversary of the Death

In the year or so after the death, it is very compassionate to be aware of the date and to send a card and/or flowers acknowledging the death to the grieving family. However, it may not be necessary to continue sending cards, letters, or flowers and to call after more than a year or so.

That being said, the problem with the anniversary of a death is that it is utterly personal and unique for each person. Some families do expect that close relatives will send a card every year on the anniversary of their loved one's death. There are several ways to view this. At some point, it is important for friends and family members to be able to move forward without making the date of the death a time shrine for the rest of everyone's life. Sometimes, a milestone of healing can be that the death date passes, and you may eventually acknowledge it only briefly or not at all. This is not disrespectful—merely a measure of your healing. Sometimes it is acceptable to be forthright and to ask the family what their preferences are. Some families are hurt when people do remember, and some are hurt when people do not remember. The only way to resolve this is simply to ask them what they would like.

Close relatives need to ask specifically what the family would like. Some people want to discuss the death with someone with whom they feel comfortable, going over every detail, every emotion. In some cases, it is a facet of healing for the person to return to his or her most profound feelings about the person on that day. Mostly, this lasts only a few years. If it goes on for more than five years, it is possible that the person is not facing the requirement to release attachment and may, in fact, be holding on emotionally to the person who has died.

For the grieving person, the anniversary day can be a time of extra prayers for the loved one. Sometimes letting go means overlooking the symbolism of the specific day. The life they had with the person is what matters—not necessarily the date the loved one died.

Miscellaneous Tough Times

What do you say to people who have not heard about your situation? What do you do about restaurants or places where people expect to see you with the person who died? What do you do about people whom you meet who ask you about the person in your life who has died? Tell them so. If they want to know what has happened, tell them. Your openness will help you and help them understand how you are feeling.

Tell people what happened in as matter-of-fact manner as possible.

If you are able, be dispassionate about it. It happened. The person is no longer here. Ask them to understand. Accept the hugs that are offered. You may find that frequently they will tell you that something similar has happened to them. Do not shy away from these moments. As you accept people's compassion, these moments in a wonderful way are helping both of you heal. This also helps you to understand that, on some level, everyone is grieving something and that, although you may often feel alone in your personal grief, you are not alone in the massive aggregate of those people on this Earth who are grieving many, many things.

The Peculiar Reactions of Friends and Family

Often when there is a death, people have some rather peculiar reactions. Some people feel that death is contagious, even if it is an irrational thought, based on the cause of death, but they think this, nonetheless. To this end, they will not allow their children to visit a family that has experienced a recent death or play with that family's children.

Some people feel that the pain of a grieving person is so great that they cannot face him or her and will avoid this kind of situation at all costs. The most common example is bumping into someone at the grocery store. If a friend sees a grieving friend or neighbor, often the person will quickly go down another aisle or leave the store so he or she will not have to "bump into them" and then not know what to say.

Widows frequently notice that couples they have been friends with for years will simply stop asking them over to dinner or to go on outings. This practice further isolates the widow from the support she needs most at that time.

Some people like even numbers at dinner, and a single, widowed person creates awkwardness at a dinner—or so is the perception.

Certain friends and relatives go to the opposite extreme of dwelling on the death or focusing on what they perceive the grieving person did wrong. They make it very difficult for a grieving and healing family to actually heal. When they try to detach themselves from this negative person, often the family rumor mill begins to grind, and the problem just becomes worse. These friends or family members are truly foul weather friends, and often you just have to avoid them.

The majority of people just do not know what to say when someone comes back from having buried a loved one. They do not know how to respond no matter how long it has been. They stumble over their words, say the wrong thing, or appear cold. They want their friend back. They want things to go back to the way they were before the person in your life died. They simply do not understand that everything has changed and that they have to change, too. Nothing is the same, and yet all the players have to return to the sameness of the mundane duties of living life.

You, the grieving person, have to help them by seeking them out and by asking them how they are. You have to open that conversation, get it started, and allow the other person the opportunity to figure out how to relate to you again. If you are having a bad day, then you can say that you are having a grief moment and would they please be patient. This really helps everyone learn from the process.

Perhaps if you can look at the grief event as a tremendous process of learning, then you can look at everything with different eyes, then you can finally dry your tears and begin to re-chart your life. Your patience with even the emotionally clumsy friend or family member will pay off in the end by enabling everyone to rebalance their feelings and their lives.

6

THE HEAVEN WORLD: DEATH AND TRANSITION

> ... that [which] we see manifested in the material plane is
> but a shadow of that in the spiritual plane ... that as called
> *death* ... is only a transition ... through God's other door ...
> **Edgar Cayce Reading 5749-3**

Dying in a State of Grace

What is grace? What is a state of grace? What is amazing grace?

Grace is an emotional place or state of peace, joy, hope, and mindfulness. It can be reached by any soul at any point in life. It is especially helpful if this state is reached long before death. There will be a tremendous benefit if this state can be reached and maintained during the death process.

What is so special about grace? Grace is that totally unique quality of trust that places us deep within the oneness of love and communion with God. There is no fear, shame, sin, guilt, pain, agony, regret, resentment, or torture in a state of grace. They are mutually exclusive. Where even one of these dark feelings exists, grace cannot be. Dark feelings look like heavy black soot in the etheric dimension. Dark feelings create heaviness within the soul, which, not only weighs down the soul, but also slows, inhibits, and delays progress in the soul's sojourn in the heaven world.

Whatever types of life people have lived, if they are at peace with themselves, those around them, and the world as a whole as they near the energetic end of their life, then they will die in a state of grace. To transfer the energy of the soul from a dense mortal body to a place of peace and light is to enhance a soul's travels through the dynamic of the heaven world. This is amazing grace.

How do you reach a state of grace? It is done by releasing as much as you possibly can of those dark, terrorizing feelings of fear, shame, sin, guilt, pain, agony, regret, bitterness, resentment, or torture. Seek forgiveness for all that you may have done in your life and forgive all those people who may have intentionally or unintentionally hurt you in this life. This very simple process is enormously freeing and begins to pave the way to grace. Realize that every single thing that has happened in your life has occurred for your highest good, no matter how painful it has been. This is a tremendous aspect of faith because it allows you to truly trust in the process of eternal life.

Another aspect of grace at the point of death is the relinquishment of the grasping heart. When you die, you are released from every person, place, or thing you have ever known or owned, loved, or hated. But some souls cling to everything, creating a state of heaviness in it. This weight impedes the process of soul evolution. You cannot evolve while holding on to the past. By releasing the emotional and material grasping of the mind, you allow yourself to feel the grace of transition and the peace of release.

Realize that life everlasting is a very long time to be bitter and fearful. Realize that mortal life is a schoolhouse of learning, and its degree is a difficult one to earn. Mortal life is dominated by an awareness of time. Time does not exist in the eternity of oneness with the Father. There is only the Now.

The moment you become aware of the concept of grace begin to be the soul of grace. Whatever comes up that inhibits this state, address it, work through it, and forgive it. It is a mighty thing to heal yourself and to allow the light of grace to fill every cell of your mortal body and all the aspects of your eternal soul. Live a life of no regret. Doing your best in every moment and looking at each experience as an opportunity for soul growth are parts of this process of becoming an evolving soul.

Life is opportunity made manifest by the Creator. When you embrace with joy this opportunity, you understand the tremendous gift you have been given. It is then that you can achieve the essence of grace. If and when you have a chance to assist others in searching for that grace within them, you would be wise not to shy away but to embrace this tremendous lesson and opportunity for service.

Death or Life or Continuation of Energy

What happens when you die? Where does soul energy go? Do you sit on a cloud and pluck a harp at death, all dressed in white? Are you alone? How does one go about understanding the amazing aspects of life after death?

If energy is neither created nor destroyed, then the energy of the physical body has to go somewhere and has to become something else. This is a law of physics. Life outside of a physical body is a very natural place. Only a small fraction of your existence is spent in the mortal body. The rest of your existence occurs in other realms. The truth is that most people really know very little of these other realms. Only the more esoteric texts discuss them, and so the mainstream knowledge is profoundly limited. And yet, when you can study these texts, they offer an amazing view of the spiritual schools souls can attend after mortal life. There are also planets to explore and jobs to do. Life outside of your concepts of this planet exists. Just because you cannot readily conceive of these higher realms does not mean that the spiritual opportunities they provide are not already on-going.

Perhaps looking at the microcosm will enable you to see the macrocosm. A leaf falls from the tree in autumn. Where has the energy of this leaf been when it returns in spring? Is it the same leaf? It doesn't matter; the energy of the tree, or soul, just keeps going, collecting wisdom and experiences all along its journey.

The Process of Dying at the Moment of Death

We are all going to experience the process of death. Yes, death is a process. Even if we live to a very old age, there will come a point either suddenly or slowly when our physical bodies will die and we will return to our previous form of souls without bodies. When you come to understand and to accept death merely as the routine process of moving from a physical body in this dimension back to pure soul in the heaven world, you will have made significant progress in advancing your understanding of soul evolution.

There is a process to dying, and it is pretty much the same for each person no matter how quickly or slowly you die. At the moment of death, the energy of the soul begins to separate from the physical, mortal body. The soul is connected to the physical body by something called the *silver cord*. This cord, which cannot be seen physically, connects the soul spiritually to the physical body. You may have heard of this silver cord when people discuss travel in dreams. It is as if your soul leaves your body to see other places and things, but this special cord always tethers your soul to the physical body. Once this cord is cut, your soul is separated from your mortal body. It can be said that the mortal body is now dead. It is interesting to note that at the moment of death, people immediately separate the words body and soul. They refer to the "remains" as the body. They refer to the soul in eulogies and prayers, as if somehow they inherently know that the separation of these two terms does truly signify the transfer of the soul into another realm.

Immediately after the cord is severed, your soul will experience your life history passing before your eyes. You will get to see your entire life, every single moment, shown to you from birth to the final mortal moment in one astounding flash of color, light, and feeling. As this is happening, all the final vital heat of the body is leaving it. The eternal and inextinguishable energy of the soul is leaving the physical body and is becoming wholly encased in the immortal soul. The soul is all that remains once the physical body is no longer needed.

It is important to note that the energy of the personality of the soul does not become saintly just because it is no longer attached to the body. The personality and characteristics of the soul are the same. The perceptions, the ideas, and the beliefs of the soul all accompany it to the next stage of existence. This is important to understand because many people believe that once a person dies, regardless of what they did or how they behaved in mortal life, any negative aspect of the person is stripped away. This is untrue. The personality remains with the soul; the soul and the personality are the same.

It is these personality traits that help determine what happens to you after physical death. This is why you say that after the mortal body dies, the soul continues to live, just in a different plane of existence. The elements that made up the mortal body are returned to be recycled into the earth, whether through burial in the earth, at sea, or through cremation. The following points illustrate the various paths a soul can take.

• Once the silver is cord is cut, people find themselves in what is often referred to as the "valley of the shadow of death" or in a dark tunnel (see *The Tunnel Effect* within this chapter). They move through this tunnel toward the light.

• If you have a strong spiritual background and believe in some type of afterlife, you will probably respond by going into the light. It takes some degree of courage to go into the light. To assist you there are always Light Beings whom you will recognize. You are never alone. However, each soul in this physical life and in the afterlife has freedom of choice. You always have the option of asking for help with your transition.

• It does appear that if souls show no remorse of any kind for the life they have led, if they are arrogant to the end, even after death, then, sadly, the light may not readily come. Most people show remorse; they are humble and "look up to the light."

• Some people fear the light because they did not always lead the kind of lives that, in their own mind or soul, would be deserving of going into this light. The heaviness of this guilt or shame may prevent their transition to the higher realms.

• This concept of the soul questioning his or her worthiness is ironically true of very religious people. These people feel that, no matter how good they may actually have been, their religion has taught them that they will never be "good enough" to be in the presence of God. That sense of unworthiness will haunt them in death and will definitely hold up their spiritual progress, however untrue it may be. *All souls are worthy of God's love and forgiveness.*

• The Light Beings who meet you are souls, whom you will recognize, such as a loved one, Jesus, Buddha, Kwan Yin, the Virgin Mary, or any other personal deity. The Light Beings may also be a beloved person such as a grandparent, sibling, parent, or even your favorite pet. It does not matter who you are; you will always be welcomed home.

• Children are frequently confused by their deaths. They do not understand that the light has come for them and that they should go into that light. Frequently, they need the living to tell them where they should go. Children who have been filled with hate or guilt or made to believe that they may be "sinners" will have difficulty accepting the invitation to move into the light. In any situation dealing with children, it is always helpful to ask for angels to come to escort them to the heaven world.

• Sadly, there is another situation in which Lower Realm Intelligences come for a particularly evil person. These were accurately depicted as the little dark guys in the movie *Ghost*, and they are just as evil as they seem. Many times, this is the afterlife the person expects and actually creates for himself or herself. If souls find themselves in this situation, they would be wise to ask for immediate angelic assistance to escort them to the correct realm of the heaven world.

Many times you feel helpless when a person dies. However, there is a tremendous amount of service that you can perform for a person who has died. You can assist the dead with their transition process by offering them prayers of hope and compassion. You can ask on their behalf for angels to guide them into the heaven world. Sometimes you may have to do this for awhile, but eventually you will find that they are able to leave. These types of prayers are reminders that no matter what a person has done, spiritual assistance is always available to them through the power of prayer. You can help. Your efforts can be exceptionally compassionate and meaningful. There are times when you can use these tools to help a person who is dying. This will greatly smooth the loved one's transition and is a tremendous service.

The Life Review

The review of a lifetime is often seen as a time of turmoil for the soul when it does not have to be. The life review is not a punishment; it is a learning tool. You are allowed to see how you spent your life and the impact you had on other people during your life. You are shown the ripple effect of your actions in the long and short term. It is rather like watching a motion picture, and each frame of the movie is a moment in your life. When you speed up the frames of each life moment, they give you an entire picture of how your life was lived. Then you, as the soul, judge yourself. There are spiritual beings available to guide you in understanding if you are willing to listen. No one judges you. No tribunal evaluates the positive and negatives of your life. You are shown that all of your experiences were just that—experiences. If you choose to learn from them at deeper and deeper levels, you make progress in your soul evolution.

The Tunnel Effect: The Valley of the Shadow of Death

Most people have come to know about the existence of something called the valley of the shadow of death. However, not everyone is too sure what that means. The valley of the shadow of death is a portal of transition. It is very easy to understand when you consider that millions of people die each day. It would be utterly unnerving to see all of those souls going to all the different places that souls go upon their death. So, in a most compassionate way, there is a process whereby, as soon as you exit the body, you move into a tunnel for further processing.

From this point, a decision is made as to where you go. Actually, your actions in life create the greatest influence on this decision. If you die in a state of grace because you believe that you are a good person and have lived a good life, the transition through this tunnel is pretty straightforward. You move through this darkness with the faith of your belief in God and a wonderful afterlife, no matter what your mortal faith or religion has been. Ironically, at the point of death, a person's specific religion is no longer relevant; there is no specific Christian, Hindu, Muslim, Jewish or Buddhist heaven. There is just God.

People who have encountered the tunnel were reminded to keep moving, not to be delayed. It seems that what creates that darkness on the other-dimensional realms is the volume of people's negative thoughts. We all have to pass through it to get to the dimension from which we will reincarnate. For some people the dimension of learning before reincarnation is the heaven world. However, if you have focused on dark thoughts and deeds, then making that passage toward the light is going to be extremely difficult. If darkness has been your norm, then, once beyond the tunnel, darkness will continue to be your norm. You can always ask for help, for assistance, and for insight; you just have to remember to make that request.

Near Death Experiences

People all over the world have had near death experiences (NDEs). While the occasional one is hellish, the vast majority of them are life-changing experiences. Dr. Raymond Moody, while studying philosophy at the University of Virginia, started a project that, when completed, contained interviews of more than one hundred people who had experienced near death episodes.

The majority of the NDE survivors Dr. Moody interviewed *knew*, without a doubt, that they were loved without condition by a force greater than themselves—God. They knew they were an integral part of this universal source of love. This powerful sense of love, they said, was not dependent upon anything they did or said—it simply was a *fact of consciousness*. The most important lesson they learned from dying was that their purpose in life was to go about the business of loving others unconditionally just as they themselves were loved. Dr. Moody said if every human being on Earth acted with that simple principle of unconditional love, then we could truly have a heaven on earth.

This message of love is perhaps the most important facet of knowledge that comes out of NDE research. The extent of our spiritual growth, development, and evolution—in this world as well as in the next—is measured and is dependent upon our willingness to manifest unconditional love towards our fellow human beings.

Dr. George Ritchie, the first NDE person that Dr. Moody interviewed, went on to conduct his own research in the field. As Dr. Ritchie illustrated, the souls that find themselves in the shadow lands or the earth-bound realms after death are not being punished or condemned by any force or power except of their own making. The *inner life* creates the *outer world* of our existence after death. If we have spent a lifetime holding grudges, harboring resentments, being prejudicial in our thinking, acting out of jealousy or hate or malice, those thoughts collectively form the building blocks that create a home in the shadow lands, the hellish realms. In accordance with universal law, that which we think, we become; and that which we build, we move into. Edgar Cayce, one of the most famous and well-documented psychics of the twentieth century, gave the following answer to a question posed to him in a reading where he defines the workings of this universal law in short order:

(Q) Where do I go from this planet?
(A) Where thou art preparing, and what thou art building.

1219-1[2]

This information has been borne out by thousands of near death experiences. People changed forever after their brief sojourn in the heaven world. Many started on a spiritual path that has enabled them to help others and to create a sense of love, hope, and joy.

What was it like for some of them? How did they travel? Many felt and heard a rushing sound—a sound that seemed to consume them as they traveled through darkness. Many found that they had no fear of this darkness and that it had a comforting quality to it. Some heard bells, while others heard choirs singing, welcoming them home. For those who felt themselves moving toward the Heaven world, they experienced a sense of anticipation for the reunion they inherently knew would be coming soon. There was also a sense of lightness, as they were no longer encumbered by the physical body. This was especially true of souls who may have been obese, overweight, or whose body had been diseased and in pain. The sense of freedom from the body was an almost indescribable pleasure.

Other souls described a fantastic light—a light so bright that many of them were convinced that it should have felt blinding to them, and yet it didn't. The light welcomed them home, made them feel safe and secure, and filled them at once with a pleasing sense of love and of delightful hopefulness.

Whom did they meet? Some met Christ. Others met people whom they had respected in mortal life. These souls could have been relatives, teachers, or friends, while others met Light Beings or angels who spoke to them, advised them, and explained to them how they came to be having such an amazing conversation and sojourn in the heaven world.

People who have had near death experiences were sent back for a wide variety of reasons. Universally, their jobs on earth were not finished, and they had messages for friends and family members. Other travelers were counseled about their desire to return to the heaven world and why it would be better for them to remain in physical bodies for the remainder of their physical lives for the service they would now be able to perform. Still others were offered a glimpse of life after mortal life and how much better a mortal life they could be living.

Of course, it always begs the question: why did these people get to have these experiences, while other people make the complete transition unto death? Only the karmic path of that soul can bring balance to the answer. Some people need the experience of completing mortal life through death, and others need the experience of returning and living mortal life differently.

Many people who have an NDE return to mortal consciousness to find that they are never the same. Some do not ever want to return to the world of physical existence. Others are sent back while some ask to return. Many return with enhanced psychic abilities. These abilities are not gifts, for the soul is responsible for their use or abuse. Some people are subject to ridicule from friends and family members who do not believe them. Others live a slightly resentful life and long to return home to that place of profound love and light. Finally, a few understand the opportunity of the experience and use the new ability in a karmically correct way, enhancing this ability by study and diligence in learning. Some stay connected to higher beings and radiate happiness and joy, which is perhaps the reason for the experience in the first place.

What Is It Like in the Heaven World?

We all come from the heaven world and the world of other dimensions, but we do not consciously remember them. When we are born, a "veil" comes down upon our conscious memories so that we can be more fully integrated into mortal life. This is why we do not remember the heaven world. Also, the purpose of the veil is so that we do not dwell on what we have come from; instead, we can focus on why we are in the physical world of life on Earth. We are fortunate that some people have had NDEs which allow them to enter the heaven world for a brief period of time and to return to share their experiences. During the NDE they are considered clinically dead, which is why their consciousness travels to the heaven world and returns; but the silver cord in these cases has not been cut, so they are not really dead. This trip to the heaven world may be to reassure people or to offer them the opportunity to cease fearing death or to enable them to return with a message for others about life after death.

Generally, they tell us that the heaven world is a place of divine love. It is hard for us to remember this most wonderful place, for the veil that prevents remembrance is strong. But for those who have had NDEs, visits to this realm are remarkable. As mentioned earlier, one of the things that you learn is that you can create certain realities regarding what will happen to you after death. Frequently, the consciousness that you create follows you into the afterlife. Your religious beliefs have a profound influence on what actually happens after death. The following is the story of a woman who was very much a born-again Christian. She believed that only a few people who were "saved" would go to heaven.

> He told us that while the grandmater [sic] was still on earth, she reckoned, same as a lot of people do, that she and a few other people were going to be saved. "And now. . . . she lives in a world of thoughts which she and others have created by their own fallacious convictions. In our Father's house are many mansions." The grandmother was in a thought-form dimension where she literally was singing hymns around a large throne with others of like-mind. If any spirit guides or angels came to try to get them to ascend to a higher dimension of consciousness, the grandmother and the others would scream in horror, presupposing that the visiting spirit was a demon or someone sent from hell. She believed this because only those in her realm were the

souls who were "saved." The rest of the world, in their belief, had been sent to hell! [3]

Many people who have had NDEs have returned to consciousness
with wonderful and amazing descriptions of what life is like in this
heaven world as seen in the following depictions:

> I was transported (how I do not know) to another Place,
> another Sphere, another "mansion" in this world . . . Suffice
> it to say that suddenly and immediately I was conscious of
> being in a great "atmosphere" of learning. I realized that I
> was in a university; yet it was much more than that, for
> there were Halls of Learning and a pervading atmosphere of
> Thought which thrilled my soul and satisfied a deep yearn-
> ing in me. There were outer courts and beautiful vistas of
> gardens, where fountains of Light played. Here there were
> many souls, groups of students, sometimes surrounding
> One who appeared to be a Teacher, intent upon His dis-
> course, or composed in deep meditation with Him . . . [4]

> "We never went into this realm, were varying at about fifty
> to 150 feet above, but this was the first place we had been
> where the beings could see us as well as we saw them. And
> the beings in this place were glowing like unto the Christ
> Himself in the amount of Light and Love they emitted. I
> called this place Heaven."[5]

George Ritchie believes that he was sent back [from physical death]
to tell others that God is a God of love, not of vengeance or punishment:

> "We are loved beyond measure, beyond our wildest
> imaginings. The Being I encountered loved every unlovable
> thing about me. And I believe He wants others to both
> know this as a *fact* and to love our fellow human beings in
> equal measure. If we loved one another as He loves us, this

material world would literally be a heaven on earth. We have the power to do this. It's all up to us."[6]

Some people are offered the opportunity to understand how much goes on after death. Souls are really active while learning, growing, and seeking enlightenment, if that is what they desire. Life in the heaven world can be busy and wonderful, indeed. One of the amazing opportunities that the heaven world offers is the ability for all new souls to see how they influenced other people, how their efforts echoed out through time and space even after death. This part of learning about the heaven world is incredibly important. It is the essence of learning how to live by understanding what happens after death. If you can appreciate that, you will get to see how you have influenced others. Imagine how much more powerfully and lovingly you would want to live life. This is what you can do to grow and to advance.

With these descriptions, you may begin to understand that you can mourn those who have died but at the same time be happy for the new experiences they are having. Life after death is truly amazing. You can deal with your own loss but rejoice for the wonderful love and learning your beloved is feeling and experiencing.

It would be wonderful to think that everyone goes to the same heaven world place, but in life and in death, we all have the experiences we need, and some of those experiences at death are not pleasant. Not all souls move directly to the heaven world. The reason is because in life we create the realities of pain, suffering, fear, and guilt. The realities that exist within us directly influence what happens to us after our soul exits the body.

> There is a level to go to when a soul crosses first over. Not all souls get to that first level immediately after death . . . Souls who commit suicide or don't believe in an afterlife can hover. Some haven't finished their business, and think they are still living [on earth]. There is a level where souls are debriefed, meet guides, meet other souls they know. A soul has a chance to stay there and they can create whatever it is that they physically miss on Earth, if they want to.

And they can stay there as long as they want to. At some
point the soul comes to an awareness that there has to be
more. It is not quite heaven. When they reach that conclusion, they are ready to move on. At these various levels there
are always tutors available. The layers/levels we are talking
about are not always successive layers. . . . So the levels are
almost as unique as the souls. At any level there are options
to get help.[7]

At any level, souls can ask for help for themselves and for the living
family and friends that they left behind. An interesting element here is
that the more remorse and love one shows at the moment of death, the
easier it is to transition into the heaven world. One of the most important aspects of this process is that no matter what level the soul finds
itself, the soul can *always ask for help*. This realization is humbling and
hopeful all at the same time. The soul is never spiritually alone. One of
the problems some people have upon the moment of death is complete
confusion. Often they do not know that they are dead. It is easy to
understand the need to show remorse if you understand that you are
dying or that you are dead, but sometimes you die so suddenly and
unexpectedly that you instantly become a ghost because you do not
know that you have died. There is some degree of lag time between the
time that you realize that you have died and the arrival of the sense of
the presence of the light. In that case, the prayers of family and friends
will be especially important in the healing and transition of this soul to
the heaven world. Again, family members can always ask for angelic
assistance to help the loved one in the heaven world.

How Religions Damage Soul Transition

Many religions do not educate people in the steps to take upon soul
transition. What do you do when death comes? Most people are not
aware of the volume of help available in the heaven world. This is a
huge disservice. Since most people do not know what actions to take
upon death, this can result in the creation of a ghost.

If religions prepared people for a graceful transition, then imagine the suffering and confusion that could be avoided once all of these souls left their bodies. Imagine the peace to be had and the reduction of ghosts on this planet. Here is an example of the effect of this belief system.

Dr. Ritchie said this realm was like a medical triage station at a hospital. All these souls were crossing over, and this was the "emergency room." This place was for determining where the souls who were crossing over should go for their future education and enlightenment:

> "The first thing that I saw there were all the young soldiers, sailors, marines, civilians that were dying in 1943, during World War II. A lot of them were "crossing over." Tragically enough, a lot of them were like me—they had been taught that when you died you slept until Gabriel came along tooting on a horn. *Nothing could be further from the truth.* This [belief] has caused more trouble! And over there the angels were having a terrible time waking these young people up because they thought they had to stay asleep until the Second Coming of Christ."[8]

Perhaps the message here is to question established belief systems. If your belief system fills you with fear of being a "sinner," of never being good enough to stand before God, then you should question this belief structure. You must do your own research. You would be wise to learn for yourself what the truth is and then follow that truth. This is the development of moral courage and inner strength. This path is not always popular or easy, but it is the truest path for each of us.

If There Is a Heaven World, Is There a World of Hell?

The more that people see themselves and others as good the easier will be their transition from the physical body into the heaven world. It is a fact that people are angry, feel hatred, and are wounded by the deeds of others, including family members, friends, and strangers. The enemy you hate can come from anywhere. Sometimes you hate, and you don't even know why you hate another person, culture, country, philosophy, or religion. You are just told that you are supposed to hate "them."

You carry the feeling of all of those types of hatreds with you when you die. Every type of hate acts like a heavy weight around your soul. Hate pulls you down into the lower astral dimensions, also known as the hells. You create your own hell. God does not send you there, nor does He create a hell to punish you. You punish yourself by your own dark thoughts, actions, and belief systems.

God is so forgiving that the opportunity to choose to stop being a hateful person is always available to you, even in the hells. You can choose to forgive and to release these horrible dark thoughts that are only poisoning you. At that point, when God offers help, you can be in a better place to accept it.

For example, sometimes a relative is one of these dark, angry persons, and you may become worried that he or she will go "to a very dark place" at death. There is often a helpless feeling that the person may not be able to shed these dark feelings. Sometimes a soul just has to go through these times to advance. Some souls want to experience everything, including darkness. Your prayers for their betterment can be very helpful to them. However, you cannot pray that they change, for you cannot interfere with their free will even when those people are in the lower astral dimensions. You can pray only that angels be sent to help them, and you can also send them your love.

Can you change the negative thoughts of others? No, you cannot. Can you change your own negative thoughts? Very possibly you can change. One less hateful person, one less angry soul, helps the whole world. If you encounter angry, hateful people, treat them with kindness. How can anyone learn kindness if he or she does not see it in others? This is The Way. If you meet people filled with hate, give them your love to warm their hearts. Every effort you make to have compassion for yourself or another is a precious work. And you can continue that work even after physical death.

Prayers to and from the Heaven World

Souls on the other side, in the heaven world, are provided with counselors who can help them with the transition from the Earth plane to the heaven world. These counselors also assist newly arrived souls help those family members remaining on Earth to understand and to accept the souls' passing with grace. This help does come in subtle ways, in ways of care and kindnesses. Sometimes a person may help you who may not know that he or she was sent to assist you, but that person appears when you need someone the most.

Prayer also works in many subtle ways. You always picture people at the age of their death. However, once they have crossed into the heaven world, they are whatever spiritual age they may happen to be. This is especially true in the case of a baby, child, or teenager. You can ask that help be given to your loved ones so that their transition will be easier and more delightful. These souls now have access to wonderful Counselors of Divine Wisdom and to beings from the angelic realms. Knowing this will provide you with a wonderful sense of peace. It also removes those helpless feelings you may have after a person has died.

You can also ask your loved one to help you with your grief, even if that departed soul was a young child or baby. Once a soul has transitioned into the heaven world, it is now in a rather unique place from which to pray. Many people do not realize that those souls who now reside in heaven can send their most heartfelt prayers to those friends and family members still in mortal bodies.

As for those other realms, souls do not have a specific age and can, in fact, send you assistance if you will only ask. In addition to asking them to forgive you for anything you might have done that was harmful, you can also seek their assistance in helping you to heal your grief at their passing. You can ask them to help you understand, on a greater level, the reason that they left at this point in their life. You can also ask your own angels for this information, as well, and together, this combination may enable you to have greater insight and understanding into the purpose and the lessons of the death of your loved one.

This concept of sending and receiving assistance from the heaven world is critically important to understand because it reminds you that death is merely a doorway to a new and different life. It is different and yet familiar. It is home to all of us, and once you are there, you can still send prayers to those whom you love whom you have had to leave behind.

You are still "alive" but in a different sense. The essence of who you were is still there. The most powerful and important thing that you take with you as you shed your mortal body is the love and experiences that you have encountered in your most recent life.

Souls send love to those who helped them and who loved them. They can send forgiveness even to those who have harmed them. Healing can continue long after death for all the parties through the very real *power* of prayer. Prayer transcends time and space and all dimensions. This is why prayer is so wonderful. So, any time you think you feel "warm thoughts" from someone who has died, perhaps you would be wise not to discount them but to embrace them for the wonderful prayers they may be.

7

GHOSTS

> Death—as commonly spoken of—is only passing through
> God's other door . . . As to how long—many an individual
> has remained in that called death for what ye call *years*
> without realizing it was dead!
>
> Edgar Cayce Reading 1472-2

Ghosts

What is a ghost? A ghost is a soul who has left the body because
the body has died. However, this soul has not moved into the
heaven world for reprocessing and education. These are souls who
often do not know that they have died. When you leave mortal
life and do not move into the light, you are referred to as a *ghost* or
as a discarnate entity.

Mortal people live in the dimension of time and space. Without
time and space, there cannot be mortal life. Time and space offer
us the opportunity to *have the time and the physical space to experience
mortal life.* When you die, you leave this dimension and enter the
next dimension or realm. Ghosts, or discarnate entities, exist in
what you would call this next dimension or nether world. In this
nether world there is no time and no space as you think of it. Most
people cannot see this dimension, but this is where ghosts exist.
From this plane of existence, the ghosts can see the living and can
often influence them. Once a ghost leaves this nether world or

dimension, it can move into other dimensions of both the heaven world and the lower astral world, or the hells. People create their own hells by their thoughts and actions.

What you do when you die has a direct effect on your soul evolution. Those souls who linger after death in this nether world dimensional plane as ghostly discarnate entities find a land of no time. They forget to notice that nothing changes for them. They never age, never feel pain, and never grow. In fact, they never change the clothes they died in. They do notice that no one hears them except the occasional mystic or psychic medium who may try to communicate with them. Many of these ghosts create havoc wherever they go. They may use energy to terrify the living, and their intense negativity can harm even plants and animals. Some of them move things; others play with electrical energy, and most are just generally working to get people's attention.

This havoc also creates karma. Frequently, these are souls who never gave a thought to physical death and are either quite surprised when it finally comes or are terrified to be in this nether world. They can see people, but no one can see them. Many of them become angry souls. If they were angry, vindictive, cruel people in their physical body, it is unlikely that they will become positive and light filled upon their death. Many of these people show no remorse for the life they have lived. This lack of remorse draws to the soul a unique brand of karma and experience, a rather unpleasant kind at best. People who commit suicide can also become quite confused in the netherworld. These souls, for the most part, are very sorry for the hurt they have caused.

People who die suddenly often end up as ghosts, at least temporarily. Once they come to understand that they have died, they usually move on or "cross over," when the light presents itself to them. In some unusual situations, they can also learn spontaneously by watching another soul move on. The karma of the individual soul alone determines whether or not the light appears for this soul spontaneously. Again, remorse seems to be the key, as well as a sincere desire to atone for actions done in the physical body.

Understanding That the Dead Grieve

When people die, they leave everything they have ever known and loved in mortal life. Some souls find separating from these things exceptionally traumatic, and for that reason they may linger as ghosts. They cannot bear to leave certain people, places, and things. Some parents literally haunt their children, even their adult children, because they cannot bear to be away from them even in death. Some angry people realize that they wasted their life in anger. Some grieve that they never told certain people how much they loved them and the living didn't get the chance to say good-bye to them. Others grieve the focus of their life, often wishing they had done things differently, such as having children or loving more. Many people wish that they could have lived their lives more passionately. This concept of living a more passionate life reminds you to do just that and not wait until death to discover how much better a life you could have lived.

If people die suddenly and feel that they had many more things left to do in their lives, they grieve the suddenness of their own passing: *I have children to raise, a husband to go back to, a job to do; my family needs me*; or *how tragically I died! I can't believe I have been murdered! How could this happen?* If the person has been a victim, if there is anger, then once out of a physical body, it is difficult to transmute that personal grief. This also helps to explain why so many people become ghosts. They grieve for themselves, their families, their loved ones, their dreams and ambitions. They grieve the fact that they have to go through the reincarnation cycle again. This grief can be evidenced by several situations:

• If the soul has deep regret concerning the place where he or she died, which would be a tremendous attachment, then the soul can become a discarnate entity or ghost, and just "hang around" that location. Some entities become mischievous ghosts, moving things around and making noise, while others are especially dangerous ghosts, creating fear in the living.

• If the soul was a mother of young children, she may grieve the feeling that she has abandoned them. This feeling could also be true of a young dad. Both souls regret that they will not be there to see their children grow up. Others may grieve the fact that someone else will raise their children.

)sts regret the fact that they committed suicide. Once , they can see the hurt that they have caused their friends and fam..... nd they mourn their decision to die.

• Some souls are very angry and regret that they did not hurt people enough. Their vicious personalities do not leave them at death but continue into the afterlife.

• Some elderly souls grieve that they felt they were a burden to their children and family. This sense of being a burden could also come from a soul who spent much of his or her life ill.

• Some souls who die suddenly at a young age regret that they will not get to live the life that they had anticipated. They grieve for the mistakes or the reckless actions that caused their deaths.

• Some souls grieve for the way in which they died. If they were murdered, it is a terrible feeling for them to see their bodies in such condition.

• Some souls who die of drug overdoses grieve for the pain that they caused their families and for the life they feel that they wasted.

No matter how people die, you can help them even in death. Your prayers act like a cleansing, healing rain on their souls. Your prayers for them light their way. Your forgiveness for the lives they have lived helps them, no matter when they died.

Perhaps understanding that you are the same in life as in death will offer you greater incentive to live a better life. The more you can open yourself up to dying in a state of peace, grace, and love, no matter the method of death, the more you will advance in your soul evolution. Perhaps you will not grieve so much at your own death. When you can do this, your process of physical death can be less stressful. When you can accept all of these facts, perhaps you can then choose to live your life differently by making sure that love dominates your life.

Are You Different After You Die or Transition?

The dynamic of the soul does not change at the point of death. A cruel, vicious murderer, who shows no remorse in life, will likely show no remorse at death. The energy, the personality, and the consciousness of souls do not change just because they are not in a physical body. On the contrary, many vicious, horrific ghosts were murderers in their physical life. Many psychics have encountered these often dangerous, discarnate intelligences and have had to deal with their vicious attacks on the living as well as on their own person. The psychic can and usually does request help from the higher realms in dealing with this difficult type of soul. It is wrong to leave it in its present location to continue to incur terrible karma by harassing and poisoning the atmosphere of living people.

On the other hand, some souls are so dedicated to service while living that they cannot let go of the people they were helping until someone comes along and literally relieves them. There is the interesting story of the psychic who was brought in to remove a ghost from a house in Virginia Beach, Virginia. The homeowner was not uncomfortable with the ghost, for the ghost was not a cruel or vicious type, yet the homeowner felt that this soul should move on. The psychic arrived and met the ghost in the house. The ghost's name was Helen Stanton, and outside the house were 200 Civil War dead waiting for something. Helen was a Civil War nurse whose job it was to care for these men even in death. She had been waiting for 136 years for someone to help her with all of these dead men. She would not leave them, even though she was aware that she and the men were all dead. She felt stuck because she needed help in enabling them to move on. Once the psychic came on the scene, she brought in an entire team of angelic assistants to help all of these Civil War soldiers cross over. After this was done, Helen felt that she, too, could finally leave. Within minutes they had all moved on and once again continued their participation in soul evolution. Their waiting was over.

Why couldn't these souls leave? They couldn't leave because the heaviness of war literally kept their vibration or energetic levels so low that they had trouble moving through the darkness of their death and into the heaven world. It takes a great deal of hate to kill someone, and a lot of darkness is created when you are killed violently. Both actions of killing or of being killed create a terrible heaviness in the soul. The lighter you are, the more readily you move on to the heaven world. This is why it is very important to work through the darkness within you. If you have a loved one who has died in a war or through an act of violence, it is a wonderful service to offer this soul angelic assistance in order to help the soul make that sojourn into the heaven world. Your prayers for these souls are also especially powerful in helping them.

Angels of Transition: Assisting Ghosts to Move On

Why do you think that you might need some help in removing a ghost? Can't you just ask it to leave? Can't you just tell the ghost where to go? The answer is "No, you can't." You, as a human being, seldom have enough spiritual horsepower to remove a ghost by simply asking. You need to remember that spiritual problems often require spiritual solutions. The gentle humility of admitting what you do not know and then asking for the assistance to recognize it, to understand it, and to learn it is the mark of a spiritually advanced soul. The more advanced you become, the more you will consistently ask for the help from your Higher Self, that part of you that is God, and from the emissaries of God—angels.

In the realms of the heaven world, there are all kinds of angels. Every angel has specific tasks to perform. Angels are also in a process of evolution, and the more you ask for their assistance, the more rapidly they evolve. One of their primary missions is to help you on Earth. Angels of transition are the ones you request to guide ghosts as they move to their appropriate realms.

Angels of transition are beings of service that any mortal can call upon to assist a ghost in distress. The angels of transition are emissaries of God, and they are always available to assist you. They need only to be asked for help. Once asked, angels of transition remove or escort a lost or confused soul to the heaven world. These are divine beings who have a specific mission to act as a bridge between the living and the non–living world of discarnate ghosts. Requesting their assistance will always raise the positive energy of an area. Requesting them immediately connects the requester with the divine. If a difficult ghost is haunting a family, all the family members will need to ask for this help.

Frequently, the soul of a child is completely confused and has no idea what to do upon death. These child souls wander around the house where they lived or the accident site. Often it is quite awhile before they are able to understand that the light and the Light Beings are there to assist them. You can help a child or any soul who has died by asking for angels of transition to escort them to the heaven world so that they will no longer be lost or lonely. If you still feel the soul in your presence, you may have to provide quite a few prayers with your request. You must never stop praying for a transitioned soul until you feel comfortable that he or she has, in fact, moved on. If you feel at peace for the soul, it is very probable that he or she is at peace in the heaven world.

A few months after the Oklahoma City bombing several psychics who are also mediums went there and cleared the location of all the ghosts. Since this was public property, this could be done without special permission. Many souls were sad and confused children who were waiting for someone to tell them what to do and where to go next. The work of these mediums was tremendous service, for they received no compensation other than the positive karma they incurred for the work they did.

Every single person has the right to request these divine beings, these wonderful angels of transition, regardless of faith or belief system. Ironically, no one actually has to believe in angels or ghosts to be affected by them. They just exist. Angels are there to provide service no matter what. What an amazing sense of security this is for all of us!

As you have read before, angels of transition are special beings whose task it is to assist either a soul who may be stuck in the nether world or one who has lead a dark life and needs help transitioning to the heaven world for soul education and assistance. The reason that asking these special angels for assistance is so powerful is that no mortal person can know exactly which realm any departed soul should enter. The physics and the karma attached to that specific transition are beyond mortal knowledge. The point is that when you ask for help, you can receive it on behalf of any soul who has died. Your positive intention of service is the most important energetic element of the request. It is important to remember that one of the most compassionate acts any mortal person can perform is to assist a ghost or discarnate entity to the heaven world.

Finally, once a request has been made to the angels of transition, it is wonderful to send gratitude to them, thanking them for their service. Gratitude and prayer will also help to heal whatever caused the ghosts to come to a location in the first place.

What Environmental Factors Create Ghosts?

Certain unique factors create the conditions wherein a ghost may linger and some things actually attract ghosts. Understanding these more esoteric elements may help you to avoid unpleasant situations.

If you are ever in a position to remove a vicious soul, you will be required to call in help from the heaven world in the form of Archangels or unique angels, called Spiritual Police to remove a difficult soul to the appropriate realm. Asking the soul to leave and burning a little sage is worthless. These unsavory souls are persistent and stubborn; cleansing their location requires horsepower. Another powerful tool is simply to visualize a "salty rain" coming down on your home and property. Salt cleanses, even in the other dimensions.

Some ghosts haunt a location and create an unsettling level of fear in the living especially in a house where a person or persons were murdered. It is interesting to note that in some states it is a legal requirement to disclose that someone died or was murdered in a house prior to sale. This type of haunting creates a level of "fogging," which means that the living person cannot think clearly. The "fog" of the ghost can be unnerving to the person. In this situation, removal of the ghost can be tremendously beneficial for the householders. Again, the use of the visualized "salty rain" is extremely helpful.

In another situation, a ghost who abused drugs, alcohol, or tobacco in life will be seeking those addictive feelings again. This type of ghost will be hanging around bars looking for a mortal person who is also addicted to drugs, alcohol, or tobacco. Once the ghost finds that it is in resonance with this heavily addicted human, it may parasitically haunt this person for a long time. In this case if the living "host" gives up alcohol, tobacco, and drugs, many times the ghost(s) will also and leave.

Certain videos and other types of games that take people into an active, on-going, often violent fantasy role may attract ghosts. The reason why violent video games, fantasy roles, and magic spells are dark and heavy is because they create an eerie, and often very evil, environment. Once a person changes this environment to one of happiness, light, prayer, and cleanliness, then ghosts often become very uncomfortable and simply leave.

Methods of fortune telling using cards and board games often attract very mean, angry, and vicious ghosts. The ghosts play games with the living by tricking the living into believing that they [the ghosts] are some powerful spiritual being from the great beyond, when actually they are common ghosts with a malevolent intention.

Certain books purporting all types of magic spells used to influence other people may open the door to all types of ghosts. The spell seekers and users may have no idea that they are creating an often dark, foggy world for themselves. One of the by-products of this type of "fogging" is the feeling of clutter in a home. There is also the feeling that the house is not clean. Ghosts leave an invisible, black, sooty type of residue that makes everything feel dirty. Often, no matter how many times people vacuum their homes, if the house is haunted, it will never feel clean. Once the ghost is removed, the home will almost instantly feel fresh and clean again.

So, to avoid attracting ghosts, use positive prayer, avoid violent video games, fortune telling tools, and magic spell books. Also avoid the heavy use of alcohol, drugs, tobacco, and prescription drugs.

Contacting the Soul After Death

Frequently, family members feel powerless when a loved one dies because death seems permanent and the soul seems extremely distant. This is why people say that they have "lost" their husband, child, or parent, but no one is lost. Grief is painful, but it does not have to go on forever. If you loved them in life, you can still love them deeply in death. However, for some people, this is not enough, and they develop a strong desire to contact the soul after death through the use of a medium. They want to know if this person is okay, afraid, alone, or feeling bewildered. There is a unique form of torture for the surviving family when they face the frustration of not knowing how their loved one is doing after death.

The problem with contacting a medium is that the best ones do not advertise, and it is very difficult to know whom to trust. There are no

credentials for "mediumship" and while there are some really outstanding mediums out there, there are also some who may not be quite what
you are looking for. Perhaps there is another way to handle this. Rather
than seeking a medium, you can take the following actions:

• Ask for angels of transition to assist your loved one into the
heaven world. Ask this angel to stay with your loved one for as long as
necessary.

• Ask that the soul receive every element of kindness, care, and
healing.

• Send healing prayers to the soul for at least two to three months
to light their way. All prayers are answered in some way and prayers
sent for many months to a soul are exceptionally powerful.

• Recite the 23rd Psalm each night out loud. This blessed and spiritually powerful passage will enable a soul to know, to hear, and perhaps
to see the light that is there for it. This point is incredibly important.
This is an especially constructive action to perform, and it enables the
soul to receive wonderful help in the other realms. This passage will
also help you to begin gently the process of letting go.

• Trust that your beloved is all right. Welcome the concept that
your beloved is being welcomed home and is being enveloped in the
love and light and energy of Almighty God.

• Finally, make a request for yourself that the love and light and
energy of Almighty God completely fill you and your entire family so
that healing can take place on every level.

8

WHAT TO SAY TO CHILDREN AT THE DEATH OF A LOVED ONE

For life and death are one, and only those who consider the experience as one, may come to understand or comprehend what peace indeed means. **Edgar Cayce Reading 1977-1**

Explaining Death to a Child

If you yourself are grieving, you may have no idea what to say to a child because your own pain is tremendous. However, you may have to find the courage within yourself to help a child with his or her pain. Depending on the age of the child, you will want to take extra care in what you are saying because whatever you do say is going to have a long-term impact on this child. The subconscious of a child is going to believe what you say because you are the adult. So, if you want your child to be unafraid, you must be extremely mindful of the words that you choose.

The world looks black and white to children—things are either good or bad. Children judge everything in this mindset. To them, life is relatively simple. Death is difficult for them to comprehend. This difficulty carries on well into their teenage years.

The following rules were gleaned from conversations with children who had experienced the death of a grandparent, parent, sibling, or friend in their lives. These children are now doing well in their adjustment to the situation. The encouraging part of all this is that children can heal. Trauma does not have to be permanent; living and loving can be normal for them again.

Cardinal Rules for Working with Any Child About Death

These rules are universal. They can be applied to speaking with adults, too; but children are the most important focus of this discussion. Some aspects of this material are obviously age dependent, but for the most part, all rules apply. Remember that death shakes the foundation of children. This foundation must be made whole again, and you can help them do this.

- You must take your time when you speak to children. Never rush.
- Get down on their level physically. Sit them in your lap. Sit on the floor if you have to, and look up at them. Remove the physically intimidating aspect of your size so that the child can really hear you.
- Use simple words of explanation.
- Looking at a child in the eye when you speak to him or her establishes trust. You communicate to the child that you are brave because you are looking at him or her directly in the face.
- TELL THE TRUTH. Lying to children to shield their feelings leads to terrible feelings of mistrust later on. For example, the parent who tells a child that this injection won't hurt (when it actually does) causes the child immediately to distrust what this parent says.
- Allow them to cry. *Never* tell a child to be brave and not to cry. This is simply cruel. Denying an emotion is never good for anyone. Allow the child to express grief as much as he or she wants.
- Tell them that it is normal to cry. Tell them that adults cry, as well; it is okay to cry when you are sad.
- Tell them that, even though you both are sad now, you both will be okay later on. This thought implies that their sadness will not be permanent.
- Allow children to talk as much as they want about the person who has died. This is a tremendously healthy release of emotion. They had a life with that person; now it is over. Talking about it creates a

change in their reality because they can come to terms with it in a natural way.

- Physically hug them often and as much as they may need it.
- If they are able to understand that death is a gateway for someone to return to God, use this explanation. Death is an opportunity to return to the heaven world for growth, healing, and knowledge. It is a special place and one that they can feel good about just knowing that their loved one is there.
- Explain that it was the loved one's time to return to God, no matter what the cause of death. This thought can help them to understand that there is a natural order of things.
- Allow children to attend the funeral and to say a last goodbye. While this is hard for the child, it does afford closure. The parent will have to decide if the child is at an appropriate age to attend.
- Give children something to do to help with the grief, like having them take charge of or assist in creating a treasure box of memories or draw/paint a picture of how they are feeling.
- Have children say prayers for their loved one each night. This practice also gives children something important to do and allows them to feel close to the person who is no longer there.
- Explain to children that it is not their fault that the person has died.
- Remove guilt from children of any age. Even if they did not always get along with the person who has passed away, explain that it is normal for human beings to disagree and that this death does not mean that they did not love this person.
- Some children may feel that if they had loved the person more, the person would not have died. Reassure children that they did provide the departed soul with more than enough love. The reason their loved one died was not their fault. Tell them that sometimes these things just happen.
- Explain that, although a person dies physically, love never, ever dies. Love just goes on forever. If this concept is hard for them to understand, offer the thought that, even though this person has died, God still sends the sun, the moon, and the stars to love us by giving us their light. Perhaps they can imagine that their loved one is a star in the

heavens. Looking up in the heavens and seeing the starlight of the one they loved may be very helpful. Love and life continue.

• Explain that it is okay to be happy, to play, and to have time when they are not thinking about this person. They still have their life to live, and so they should.

• Return them to their routine as quickly as possible. The ordinary day-to-day activities of getting up and going to school remind children that their world is still mostly stable. Changing everything is horrible for children because their emotional foundation then actually begins to crumble. You can survive an emotional earthquake if your routines are still intact.

• As parents, do not go to that emotionally toxic place where you fight or blame each other. This is emotionally catastrophic for children.

• Provide lots of physical contact; hug them; let them sit on your lap, or rock them. Just let them be with you. This reestablishes a stable world for them.

• Remind children of any age that they can always send angels and prayers to the person who has died. These two things help the person who has left and gives the surviving children a positive action to perform.

• Look at photographs of the person who has died and talk about how the children enjoyed that person during life. Hiding photos of the person who has died is extremely confusing to children. Why can't they look at this person anymore? Keep photos around to remind them of how much they all loved this person.

• Never pretend that the death did not happen; going on as if nothing happened is horribly confusing for a child. Someone you all loved died. Talk about it. Look at those pictures and never forget to keep on loving each other.

Death of a Pet

The first death experience most children ever have is with the loss of a pet. This event can be a valuable experience. It teaches impermanence—that things live and that they die. If an animal has to be put to sleep, take the child along if it is felt that this child, usually age seven or older, will learn from the opportunity. Explain what will happen to the pet. Explain that it will be painless. Tell the child that this is a natural part of life and that, although we do not do this for adults, we do help animals stop suffering when they can no longer manage their bodies.

Conduct a service for the pet. Pray for the animal and honor the memory of the love the animal gave all of your family. Just because the pet is not here does not mean that he or she is forgotten.

Ask the child to draw a picture of their beloved pet.

Plant a tree in memory of the animal so that you can teach your child that, even though something dies, life can still continue.

It is a good idea to get another pet reasonably soon, within thirty days, if possible. Children have much love to give, and giving it to an animal is really important for their emotional development. They also receive unconditional love in return.

Let children grieve their pet. If they ask you questions about this death, then answer them honestly. All human beings want to explore the concepts of death so that they can understand living. The polarity of the concepts of life and death is what enables us to value life as much as we do. This is why you are wise to be careful with each other and those creatures you love.

Explaining Death by Age

Ages 2–5

From ages 2 to 5, tell children that something has happened to their loved one or pet.

Then explain to them that what happened was very big and that it caused this person or pet to die.

Explain that this person or pet is not able to come back to see them. Children may scream and cry or have a rather delayed reaction. Let them respond in whatever way they wish. Hold them. Love them. Do not judge their physical reaction.

Explain that the person has gone to a new home, the home of God. It is important to a child to have some frame of reference as to where this person is now. Explain that the angels are taking care of the loved one and that this person has to spend time there to learn and to grow.

If the child wants to know whether the person hears prayers, say that all prayers are heard. It is also important to explain that praying for the person to return is not something that can be answered in the way the child thinks. Such prayers are difficult, because they indicate that the child is not accepting the fact that the loved one has died and is not returning. It is important for the child to understand that the person cannot come back, no matter how much the child asks for this in prayer.

Where possible, explain that souls who have transitioned into the heaven world do send prayers to those souls whom they have left behind in the physical world. You can often feel their love for you in subtle ways. If the child wants to know why he or she (the child) cannot hear the prayers of the person who died, it is because the prayers are done silently and at night and are offered while the child is sleeping in order to shower the child with love in the sleep state. Love transcends death. Love that has transcended death is often best expressed by prayers given and received by those who still live in a mortal body and by those residing in the heaven world.

If they want to write a letter to the deceased, that is okay. Explain that this letter cannot be mailed, but that, by writing their thoughts down, in a funny kind of way, the person can hear them in heaven.

If children want to know what heaven is like, explain there are wonderful things there. Whatever they can imagine is what is there—their pets, sometimes their toys, and a scene which is beautiful and full of love.

When children tell you that they miss the physicality of the deceased, the touches, and the special smell, tell them that you miss these things, too, and maybe you both need a hug. It is normal to miss those things. At this age it is not necessary to go into lengthy explanations.

Fears of a parent dying are normal after they have experienced the death of someone else, especially if the death was one of the parents. This fear may linger for quite some time. Only time and a steady hand will help a child overcome this insecurity. If a grandparent or sibling died, then the fear is that there can also be a loss of a parent. Allow the child to tell you about these fears. Listen patiently. Your patience helps reestablish the feeling that this child's world can return to a stable place and that their feelings matter. A stable world makes for a stable child.

If the loved one committed suicide, do not discuss the details. Explaining death is hard enough; explaining that the person did it deliberately will be beyond the child's comprehension and may cause unnecessary guilt and insecurity. Eventually, the child will have to be told what happened, but that day is much later on for someone of this tender age.

Ages 6–12

Children of this age group are much more capable of understanding that death is a part of living. They have experienced a little more of life and are better able to understand the big picture. Up to this age, they may have already experienced the death of a pet. These children are in school and will be exposed to the trials of facing other children after this trauma. Children will need help with this. You can speak to their teacher and explain what has happened, including the death of a pet. Have the teacher explain to the class that there has been a death. Give the classmates permission to talk to your child about what happened. Talking about the event removes the trauma by simply making it more familiar. It happened, and it is a fact. Ignoring it or even refusing to discuss it creates a terrible sense of fear and isolation for the child. Giving him or her permission to discuss it with school friends is enormously helpful. The child may cry easily in school or appear very melancholy. The child may be especially sensitive to any situation that comes up. While these reactions are not true for all children, they are for some. Remember that the other children are also learning from your child's experience. The better you handle this, the easier it is for everyone.

Schoolmates may ask your child the following questions:

"What happened to the person?" Other children want to know the details of what the child knows. Brief your child that these questions are coming and tell your child what is okay to say. A prepared child will handle things with confidence, despite feelings of pain. A child who may be surprised by a classmate's questions may feel inadequate.

"What were you doing when it happened? Where were you?"

"Did you cry? Did other people cry?"

"Did you see it happen?"

"How did you feel when this happened?"

"What thoughts were you thinking when they told you that your sibling, or parent, or grandparent wasn't coming back?"

"Did they leave you anything? Did you inherit their things?"

If the person who died was someone who played with this child, be it grandparent, sibling, friend, or parent, there will naturally be a sense of loneliness. The child is going to have to chart a new path without this person. Playing without the loved one for the first time will be tough. Guide your child through this; play with him or her yourself, or ask a trusted relative to do this too. Play is a crucial step in healing. Play enables a child to feel normal again and helps him or her to realize that some aspects of life can go on as they did before. Not everything has to change.

You can also explain that it is okay if the child finds himself or herself playing and not thinking about what happened. Every minute does not have to be spent dwelling on this death. You can have a respite from it and remember what it feels like to laugh out loud and to giggle.

If it is a sibling who has died, remember that children may suffer from survivor guilt. Why did they get to live and why did their sibling have to die? If you tell them that you do not know, then that is the truth. You have to explain that sometimes things just happen. If you think that they can begin to understand this, tell them that sometimes you may not fully understand why something happens the way it does, but that over time, you will come to have a greater understanding of the events in your lives. Sometimes you have to be very patient and trust that those answers will eventually come to you.

Don't forget to laugh at the funny things the person used to do. Talk about the person often with your child. Be comfortable with this.

If you are grieving, too, you just have to be aware of how much extra energy will be required to work through this challenging time for both of you. If you do not feel up to helping your child with this grief, ask someone competent to help you. Feel free to cry in front of your child. You or other family members are also grieving, and your child needs to know that you really miss that person, as well. You will find that you just need to help each other.

This age is also still too young to explain suicide.

Ages 13–20

This age group is much more capable of understanding a death. While the same rules apply to them, you can and will go into more detail with them. This includes telling the truth about the suicide of a family member, if this is the case.

Never talk down to a teenager.

Never be condescending.

Never assume that he or she won't understand.

You would be wise to think the best of your teenager.

If you are grieving, too, ask your teenager for help in return. Allow young adults to rise to any occasion; universally, they are just waiting for the chance to be a wonderful person to you. Believe in them.

The effect of death on this age group, however, is just as traumatic as on the earlier ages. Teenagers are discovering who they are, who they want to be, and how they will address life. A traumatic event at this age will affect them. It can cause just as much fear in them as a child of a younger age. However, it is also an experience that they can triumph over and appreciate.

This is the age when, tragically, many of their peers either consider or go through with suicide. Teenagers are frequently depressed. Suicide may be contagious; if one person does it, perhaps others will, too. One high school junior had seven friends commit suicide within one year and actually attempted it herself until she finally got help. Parents are usually woefully unprepared to help a teenager with the suicide of a friend.

If your teenager has a friend who has committed suicide, take time to have a serious talk about it, more than once. If you see your son or daughter's grades fall and they seem sullen, you must talk to them in a sincere manner. If they will not talk to you, bring in someone they will talk to. Sometimes you have to get yourself out of the way. It doesn't matter who the messenger is, as long as teens get the message.

If a family member dies, your teenage son or daughter may need more help than you can provide. Consider asking a family member to assist him or her if this is a really capable person or else find a grief counselor.

Never be afraid to discuss a death with teenagers. This discussion, above all else, is what will enable them to heal. If you do not have an answer to a question or an issue that he or she poses, then research it together. Whatever you do, never make this teenager feel guilty about a death.

Teenagers should see family members grieve. On your more difficult days, ask your son or daughter for a supportive shoulder to cry on. All players in the drama of a death will need help, and at various times let them know that you all play those roles of helper and "helpee."

The bottom line is that the more honestly you approach the situation, the easier it will be to heal.

Funerals

There are several views about allowing a child to attend a funeral. Again, it is up to the parent(s) to decide whether or not a child is at an appropriate age to attend a funeral. Based on conversations with children who lost family members, it meant a lot to them to be able to see that there truly was no life in the body of their grandparent, sibling, or pet. This really seems to help them adjust to the absence of the physicality of the person. If their last encounter with the person was when the loved one was happy and smiling and then someone said that the person had died, there is an intellectual disconnect. They have to see for themselves that the person really is dead. Now they can be at peace.

It is also a good idea to ask children if they would like to say a few things about what they remember regarding the person who has died, perhaps the funny things they recall about the person they love.

When a cremation is the chosen method of handling the remains, work with the child, if it is possible, to design a ceremony to release the ashes at sea or into the ground to create a positive feeling about this aspect of letting go.

Children are surprisingly comfortable with the concept of cremation. If someone is worried that the child will not understand, it is important to explain that the body is simply an empty shell; seeing this firsthand at the funeral home will really help the child to understand. The loved one is not in that body. Returning the body to ashes is a natural part of the cycle of life.

Keeping conversations clear, honest, and simple is very powerful. Tell children in advance what will be taking place at the funeral and gravesite ceremonies. Let them know that people will be crying and talking. If they are uncomfortable, assign a friend or relative to take the child to a place of peace and quiet.

Help them to say prayers for the person at the funeral and let them have a private goodbye away from the eyes of other family members.

Be aware that well-meaning friends and relatives may say inconsiderate things to your child. Be alert to these things. Sometimes the words a well-meaning friend speaks can be very hurtful to the child and may linger in a child's head for a long time. Even overhearing those words is enough to cause a child to feel unreasonable guilt. Always remind your child, no matter what the age, that the person who left really loved him or her.

Grief Counseling for Parents

Many parents become depressed as they struggle through their own grief. They think that they can just "handle it themselves." They mistakenly believe that they can see all the aspects of their own grief and work through it on their own. All people who are grieving can benefit from professional help, even if it is just to talk about it.

The parent who endlessly struggles in the heartbreak of depression is of no value to his or her children. If you are drowning yourself, how can you possibly help your child? The airlines explain it the best when the flight attendant announces that in the event of an air catastrophe, place the mask over your own nose and mouth first and then try to help your children. The parent who is gasping for breath and passing out can't possibly help anybody.

There are parents who lose a child and heal. They stay married to each other and provide a strong, stable environment for their remaining family to live and grow. They help each other. They get help. They acknowledge their own limitations, and then they begin to heal. They come to understand how much this child gave them, and somehow a new appreciation for the experience emerges that enables them to detach from the person in a more balanced way. Families that permanently go to pieces at the death of a child have a very difficult time releasing attachment to this child and often the attachment to the guilt that goes with this death.

Many children feel personally responsible for the grief of their parents, wrongly believing that somehow they have to make it up to their parents for the loss of their sibling. This is not their responsibility, and often they are not quite sure where this feeling came from, but it can be quite strong. Children like this will be sentenced to a life of guilt when they discover that they could not help their parents regain happiness.

The parents who lose a child, a spouse, or other close person and stay in endless depression, convinced wrongly that they can never be happy again, rob their living children of future happiness. It takes courage to leave this dark place, but no one ever said that parenting was easy. Parenting is excruciatingly hard when you are grieving, but your responsibilities do not leave you. They are still there. You have to live up to them, even in your darkest hour. You must get help. Once children see their parents receiving help, then family balance can be restored. Children learn that it is important to ask for help and to work through all the pain associated with the death of a loved one.

If a Child Witnesses Death

Witnessing a death is a terrible moment that is usually not soon forgotten. If a child witnesses the death of a pet or animal on the road—for example, if a car hits the animal—let the child talk about it. This is serious drama for a child, who is being given an opportunity to understand death. Do not shrink away from this discussion.

If, by some terrible circumstance, a child witnesses the death of another person or a family member, this is tremendously traumatic. The best way to heal trauma is to talk about it, over and over and over again. If you do not feel up to the task, get professional help. A clergyman may not always be the best bet for a child because a clergyman may represent too much of an authority figure. A professional grief counselor will provide better help for the child.

There are many therapies that help children who experience various traumatic events, such as a hurricane, tornado, earthquake aftermath, fire, or accident. The losses of a home through foreclosure or of the parent's job are also traumatic events for a child. Some therapeutic methods to help include writing letters, keeping a journal, drawing pictures, and play therapy. Expressing feelings is the process of releasing the trauma until it no longer resides within the child.

Is God Angry at Us?

Many children wonder if God is angry with them or is He punishing them because this loved one died. They immediately think back to a negative thing that they said to this person and wonder if somehow their statement or action caused the death. Some children wonder if God has actually abandoned them because there is so much hurt in their lives. Reassure the child that God is not angry with anyone, nor does He punish us. God loves us. This is a terrific opportunity to explain that God does not give us our pain. Sometimes experiences happen to us so that we can learn about joy and sorrow and pain and healing. By focusing on what can be learned from the experience, the event is immediately removed from the realm of punishment by God.

Never, ever let a friend, teacher, or relative say negative things to children about a recent death. Do not let people put terrifying ideas in their minds. Keep their minds open to love, happiness, and the concepts of healing.

It is important to remind children that all that is happening to them is a lesson in the process of learning about love. This thought is especially important when they feel abandoned and when the pain in their hearts will not dissipate. Rather than feel horrible forever, this is an experience that you can use for learning. It is okay to feel sad sometimes. It is also *really* okay to feel happy and enjoy friends. Giving a child permission to be happy again will be significantly helpful. The delightful laughter of your child is enormously healing.

What if a Child Is Angry at God?

Directing anger toward God is, to some extent, normal for a child. Sometimes you feel that you have to be mad at someone, and God is pretty handy. Tell the child that it is okay to be angry at God. He is so generous that He will understand that this child is simply sad.

Perhaps the child can write a letter to God and pour out his or her feelings.

You can also explain that God has welcomed your deceased loved one into the glories of the heaven world and that your loved one is receiving help and is not alone. You can also explain that you cannot always have all the things you want when you want them. You have to accept that sometimes you have to let go. You must be as gentle as you can in this area.

You can prove that God always loves us all, by reminding the child that He sends us the warmth of the day and sparkle of the starry night without end, and that these heavenly bodies shine on us always. Thus His Love shines on us always.

Explaining That It Was Just Their Time to Return to God

When you explain that a person left because it was his or her time to go, it may seem quite natural if the person were eighty–seven years old. When the person is six years old, that seems terrifying. Everything has a season. Everyone's time of living is different. Dogs live shorter lives than cats. Elephants live longer lives than mice. We all live; we are all different, and we all have our own time frame for the length of our lives. Sometimes what you think is supposed to happen does not happen, and what you believe should never happen does. Yet all things occur perfectly in the grand scheme of life.

Sometimes a person's soul gains all the experiences that it needs in seven short years or in thirty years. How can you comprehend this? How can a child understand this? You can explain this to a child, saying that the person's life was complete when he or she left. Although you had expected the person to do more in his or her lifetime, that belief was yours alone and not that of the loved one's.

Some children may be afraid that their lives may end in a very short time. Tell them that there is absolutely nothing to fear. Everything happens in perfect time and in perfect order. You can also explain that your loved one's death did happen in this perfect time so that you can now have the experience of understanding and learning about death and healing. This gives the death tremendous meaning. Death is not cruel; it is just part of living. You all will eventually be reunited in the heaven world.

Returning to God is a wonderful experience, not a tragic one. Offer a different opinion here. Yes, you see people crying, but the deceased person is in a wonderful place. You can be at peace with this concept. The tears are based on the wonder of love—not on anger at the person's departure. You are not angry at the loved one. You love the departed and the people who are still living. You simply love. The more you love, the more you heal.

Grief Waves in Children

Grief waves hit adults at awkward times. It is the same for children. When a wave hits, just go with it. If the waves keep coming months after the death, you may have to work harder with your child to help him or her release pent-up trauma.

Some children are afraid to live and are afraid that the death or accident that happened to their loved one or friend will happen to them. It is important to let your child know that there are hazards to living. You cannot avoid all of them all the time. You cut your fingers, stub your toes, get sick, or break bones. Sometimes more serious things happen. You can either decide to stay afraid or to live life all the way. This is the choice you are given. The parent's job is to help their children face the future without fear and to show courage in the face of difficulty. Children will learn how to handle other crises in their lives by watching how their parents handle this one.

After a traumatic event the hardest job for a parent is to help a child trust that the world is still safe. That reassurance takes work and does not happen immediately. Often the most powerful grief waves come at night when children are preparing for bed. The distractions of a normal day are gone, and you come face-to-face again with the reality that your loved one is really gone. There may be many tears at this time. Be extra patient during these times. Healing takes as long as it takes.

How Can Your Child Help a Sad Friend?

What do you do if your child has a friend who is really, really sad? Let's say the child has lost a parent, sibling, or pet and just can't seem to find anything to be happy about. You can assist your child through this situation by inviting the grieving child over and letting the child know that it is okay to play and to be happy while playing. Be sure to get the other parent's okay first.

Provide this sad child a happy time. If the child wants to cry, that is fine. Tell your child that he or she can be a real friend sometimes just by listening. You can't always find ways to make other people happy. Sometimes, you just have to accept that people will have sad days but that the friendship your child offers may be priceless to that sad child who may no longer feel quite so alone.

Listening

No matter what the age of your child, one of the best tools in your spiritual toolbox is simply listening to him or her. Hear the child without judging what he or she is saying. You do not always have to fix it. Some days are just difficult to get through. Say prayers together. Laugh and cry together. Go to the movies together. If you feel sad, as well, share that emotion with your child. Be an honest parent and a consistent friend. Love this child enough to show sorrow when you feel it. Let the child know that you, too, will eventually be all right. Tell children that you love them for their courage in facing this situation. Children understand courage if you explain that courage means being brave and facing something, even though it is hard. Courage builds character. Courage helps all of us know who we are.

Understand that you cannot buy things to make a sad situation happy. You cannot make the world perfect for your child. Sad things happen to nice people. Understanding this fact will enable everyone to be part of the team in healing your sad hearts.

Love

Love never dies. Love lives forever in your heart. Love with all your heart every day. Never be afraid to love someone because that person is going to leave you. Love all the more because each day is an opportunity. You must not shut down your love for your child or let your child shut down his or her love for anyone else. You must be the example. Help your child be the example for others by allowing this child to help other people, even you. When you and your child are filled with love, then you both can begin to smile through your tears, remembering the love you shared with the one who is not here. You can smile more in that memory, and then one day, you will only smile and there will be no more tears. That is the day when you and your child will know that you have both healed.

9

UNDERSTANDING AND ASSISTING VARIOUS TYPES OF GRIEF

In that moment—as in birth, we have the beginning of an earthly sojourn, little or long as time may be—as the birth into the spiritual plane begins with the death in [the] earth plane; merely the separation of the spiritual and soul forces from the earthly connections. **Edgar Cayce Reading 900-19**

Grieving and Assisting Those Who Are Grieving

This section is designed for the person who is grieving and for the person who is assisting a friend or family member with their tragic loss. Be sure to read both parts of each of the applicable sections in this chapter. You may also want to go back and re-read Chapter Four on Grief Tools.

It is always tremendous service to help another. Even though you might be grieving yourself, you may be called upon to help a child, a parent, or a spouse. Grief is no respecter of position or level of pain. Everything you do to help yourself and another is a huge service. It is also a learning process, because, as you learn to help yourself to heal, you are also learning how to help someone else with the same issue. As hard as it is, understanding this process on deeper and deeper levels helps you to evolve as a person.

If You Are Dying—Understanding Your Own Death

What if it is you who are dying? What if you receive the diagnosis that the end is near? What if you have to face the loss of all that you have known or been connected to in this mortal life? There are many situations wherein a person must knowingly face his or her own death:

• You have been ill for a long time and have grown weary of living with the pain and have finally come to the conclusion that death is coming as your body begins to lose its strength.

• You are not feeling well and receive a diagnosis that you have a few weeks to live, and you are immediately overwhelmed with this devastating news.

• You are in some kind of an accident and realize that you are dying as the final moments come upon you.

• You are in a coma and realize that you must choose to leave or to stay.

• You are a soldier in battle, and in order to save your compatriots, you must sacrifice your own life.

All of these scenarios require a person to come face-to-face with his or her own demise. For some the passing is virtually instantaneous, while for others it is a long, protracted journey to the heaven world.

In the scenarios where death comes upon you quickly, the more profoundly you have lived with a sense of love, the fewer traumas you will suffer. It is extremely important to understand what to do when death comes, especially if it happens quickly. The more you understand about death, the more readily you can anticipate the appearance of the light and move toward it. You will also want to look for a familiar face—perhaps a family member or another loved one. No matter the method of death, you can find peace in the process after the moment of death has passed. You are simply going to walk through the door of your next moment—life in the heaven world.

If you learn that you are going to die within a short or a long window of time, then you can begin to make those preparations for death to help those whom you will leave behind. While making those preparations, it is critical to begin to grieve your own passing. You will need someone by your side who has the strength to help you through the entire dying process. It is not enough just to do the mechanical things of putting your affairs in order. You will need a person who will allow you to cry on his or her shoulder, will allow you to say how you feel, and will help you to let go of the attachment to things of your mortal life. Hopefully, this person will enable you to give away those things you know you will no longer need. This is also a part of the process of letting go.

You will also want to go through the process of forgiving all of those who may have hurt you in the past. It is important to realize that forgiving these people will set you free. You can also ask for forgiveness from friends and family members as a process of atonement and healing.

It is important to remember to love your physical body, even though this body may seem to be failing you. This body may have done all that it could to support you. Honoring the corporal body, even in death, is exceptionally powerful because it is an aspect of profound gratitude for the opportunity that this body afforded you to have mortal experiences.

If you are able, analyze all that you can about the life you are ending. What have you learned? What have you learned specifically about love? How has love changed your life? This process of dying has great potential for helping you to understand life itself. Sometimes you learn more by dying than you may have learned by living.

Remember that you will live again. Decide how you will do things perhaps better in the next life and remember what you have done exceptionally well in this life —things you will want to do again when you have your next opportunity for a mortal life. Imagine how powerful it will be to have this level of awareness prior to your physical death.

Finally, remind those you leave behind that you will be all right and that you will love them no matter where in the heaven world you find yourself. Remind them all that love transcends time and space and dimensions.

Assisting a Dying Person to Grieve His or Her Own Passing

What can you say to someone who is dying? You go to the person's hospital room, and you see him or her just lying there and involuntarily think to yourself: *Thank heavens, that's not me!* That is pity—not compassion. Pretending the person is going to get better and everything is going to be just fine is pitiful denial. Talking about mindless things helps you—not the dying person.

Compassion is standing in front of the dying person and thinking to yourself: *If I were in that bed, what would I want people to do for me, to say to me? What would bring me comfort?* Here are some ideas for helping people in the dying stages of their lives:

• If they ask you if they are dying, and it is permitted, tell them the truth and tell them that you are here to help with the dying process.

• If realizing that they are dying is cause for tears, do not shy away. Allow them the opportunity to cry. They are grieving, and this is a healthy reaction. Be patient. They will get to the other side of these tears.

• Make sure that the atmosphere surrounding dying people is as calm and as serene as possible with no arguments or shouting. Do not treat them as if they are already dead. Never speak about them in the third person when they are lying there in the bed, fully conscious.

• Make the commitment to *really listen* to the dying person. If you are there to help, you may be required to hear difficult things. Be ready to do this without judgment.

• Be patient while they talk about the grief they are feeling.

• Allow them to cry repeatedly and to grieve the loss of their own body and its deterioration.

• Tell them how much their friendship or parenting or relationship has meant to everyone.

• Be mindful that they are saying goodbye to everything known and familiar. The dying may feel a loss of everything they have ever had. They will have to grieve this situation in their own way.

• Review all the wonderful things you have done together.

• Ask if there is anything they want to talk about, or if there is anything on their minds that they want someone to know or to pass on.

- Help them with a life review. Ask them to think back to all the things they are the most proud of. Then talk about them.
- Ask if there are things that they are not so proud of that they would like forgiven. Often, the answer is yes. Advise the people that they don't have to share the details, but suggest that this is a good time to ask those people for their forgiveness even if they are not physically present or may have died.
- Ask if there are people who have harmed them and whom they would now like to forgive. Again, most people say yes.
- Ask if there is anything they want to say or want written down.
- Help them understand that you, or family, or friends will be just fine after they are gone. Tell them that they will be missed but that everyone will be sending them messages, love, and prayers.
- Ask them if they need or would like to pray.
- Ask if you can rub their feet or hands with essential oils, if permitted. Wipe their face or read to them some favorite passage as a way of comforting them.
- Bring them flowers if that is permitted.
- Just sit and hold their hand. Sometimes, dying people feel that others do not want to touch them.
- Tell them that someone will be there to meet them when they leave their body and to look for that spirit guide, angel, or predeceased family member.
- Tell them that you will always love them, now and forever.

That which you do for these people may be exactly what you will want someone to do for you. Not only is this karma in action, it is the very nature of compassion. It may take courage. So, take a deep breath and stand up to this emotional opportunity for self-growth, and be grateful to the person who is offering this wonderful opportunity to help with these intimate aspects of death.

Assisting a Person in a Coma

If you have a loved one or family friend in a coma, how can you best help the person? There are many possible reasons a person is in a long-term coma. One reason concerns the process that caused the coma in the first place; the accident or event may have literally knocked the soul out of the body. In this case, the person may not know how to find his or her body. The best way to help the person is to ask for assistance from the angelic realms to help your friend or family member find the way back to his or her body. Send powerful prayers to help light the way so the person can find the way back, as well. Also ask that healing be given to this person so that the body can literally welcome this person back into it.

There is another scenario with persons in a coma; the person has to decide whether to leave or to stay. Perhaps the person has been in this state for months, even years. If you are able, speak to the person very plainly and explain that he or she needs to make a decision about the path for this soul. Does he or she plan to stay in this body or go to the heaven world? If the person is going to stay, he or she needs to go ahead and "wake up." If the person is going to leave, you may suggest gently to him or her that it is okay to leave. Often souls find themselves in a very odd position and do not know what to do. Many of them actually want to leave, but they are torn literally between two worlds. You may give them permission to leave if you feel that you can do this. You can also ask for assistance from the angelic realms to help coma patients make their way into the heaven world.

If you are not sure how to help, say a prayer asking for divine guidance for that which will be in the best interest for this person. Be patient while you listen for the reply, because it may take time to hear it, but with diligence, you can begin to get a sense of what is the best course of action to help this person.

Death of a Twin or Multiple-Birth Sibling

The death of a twin, triplet, or other multiple-birth siblings is an utterly devastating experience for the surviving sibling(s). Twins have a unique bond that only another twin can fully appreciate. This is true for either fraternal or identical siblings. It does not matter when a twin dies; the other twin will know and that can be true even before twins or multiples are born. Very often when a twin dies *in utero*, the surviving twin may always have a longing for that sibling. Many parents never tell their child that he or she was a twin. The parents may choose to spare their child the details of the birth experience. It will not matter. The surviving twin will always know somewhere deep inside that there is a part of him or her that will always be with the twin who was not born. If a child asks whether he or she had a twin sibling, and this is true, do not hesitate to share the experience with the child. Often this information can validate the child's feelings and thus be very meaningful to him or her.

If an adult discovers that he or she had a twin sibling, then it may bring about a considerable level of healing if the twin can be encouraged to do a spiritual service that honors the sibling who was not born. This can be something as simple as acknowledging the existence of that soul, sending the soul prayers, or offering him or her flowers as a way of honoring their connection. This can be designed any way a person wants. The key factor here is to honor the deceased sibling.

If a set of twins or multiple siblings are born and all survive into childhood or adulthood, the death of any one of them will cause a very powerful grief for any or all of the surviving siblings. They will literally feel the passing of this person.

Helping them to grieve this will require the utmost compassion as any death does; however, it will be important to understand the powerful unique twin connection. It is not possible to have any appreciation for how that twin is feeling because no one from a single-child birth can appreciate the connection multiple-birth people have.

Ask them to explain, if they can, how they are feeling and what they are going through. Sometimes all you can do effectively is to listen with an open heart and to sympathize with the unique pain of their grief. It may be very meaningful to get them to tell you what it means to be a twin to that departed soul and how much the loved one meant. Sometimes putting these deep feelings into words can release the pain of the moment.

Death of a Baby or a Child

When children die, hopes and dreams go with them. There are so many emotions that they are often quite difficult to sort out. Parents feel inherently guilty that they are outliving their children, which is just not something any parent expects will happen. People around them feel a chill, a cold reality check that if this can happen to this family, then no one's children are safe. Some people actually avoid a family who has lost a child, as if death were contagious. So the emotional reactions for all the people in the drama of a child's death are complicated, often fear driven and difficult. However, no matter what your position in the scenario of the death of a child, it is important to understand how all the various players may feel.

If You Are the One Who Is Grieving a Baby or a Child

You may feel guilt that you have, in fact, outlived your child. You and every parent before you who has lost a child feel that it is wrong to outlive your children. It is important to understand that some children were meant to be here only a short amount of time and that they did not need necessarily 100 years of mortal life to accomplish their life goals. There is no guilt here; it just is what it is.

You may feel guilt that you have somehow failed as a parent to protect your child from whatever was the cause of death, even if that death was not your fault. Once beset with "what if" and "if only," these questions can lead you to a very dark place. Remember that you are a good person and that you have done the best that you could. Remember as well that people die at all stages of life. There is no guarantee of a long stretch of earthly life. You are here for as long a time as you need to accomplish your life's task. Parents cannot know how long this may be for their children.

You may feel that the death of this child was your fault. If it were truly your fault, such as forgetting that you left your child in a hot car in the summer, or if there were a shooting accident, these feelings of guilt can be healed only with dedicated grief counseling. Over time you must find a way to forgive yourself. You can be forgiven. Other people will forgive you, as well. Whatever the cause of the death, it is important to understand that death is simply a transition from one place to another and that your love for this child is not diminished by his or her sudden death.

You may grieve that you will never get to watch this child go through all the stages of childhood, adolescence, and adulthood. In a sense, you grieve for experiences that you will both miss. Voice these feelings. This grief will resound for a long time, and healing this grief will take patient acceptance of the fact that these events can now never happen. However, you can take joy in the growth stages of your other children. Sometimes, however, you just have to talk about what you are feeling at each stage of grieving.

You may grieve that you will never have grandchildren from this child. Eventually, you can come to understand that some souls were not meant to have children. Some souls are meant to live a short life to offer all the players in a family the opportunity to learn from this particular life and death experience.

You may find that you are grieving and will profoundly miss all of the charming adorable things that children say and do. You will miss these things, but it does not mean that you cannot enjoy the wonderful things that are going to happen with your other children or the children of family and friends. Of course it is not the same. The lesson is to continue to love children, no matter whose children they are.

The death of a child is the death of innocence—both the child's innocence and the tender, innocent feelings that you have for this child. The death of innocence feels like a world shattered. The feeling of safety will take patience and time to rebuild.

One of the hardest issues to heal after your child has died is fear. Even though you know that you have already lived through the worst that can happen, if you weren't fearful before, you may be now, and your job may be to learn to voice these fears. Sometimes you may fear that if this could happen once, it could happen to your other children or relatives as well. You have to be prepared that every illness or sometimes even the sound of a siren may trigger a fear reaction. Patience and reassurance are the tools that will help heal this element of grieving. Eventually, you will be able to return to that place of understanding where you know you are safe and you feel that your world will eventually come back into balance. You have to continue to trust God. You will get to the other side of this feeling.

You may feel that you are being punished for something, and this is the reason why your child died. It takes a long time to begin to understand the purpose of any death, and a child's death is especially challenging. However, every single death has a meaning, and that meaning has to be analyzed and appreciated. It is important to remind yourself repeatedly that you are not being punished, even though it may feel that way.

You may feel a tremendous emptiness in your heart, as if part of your very physical structure has died or has become numb to the rest of life. There are some parents who no longer trust love. Loving and loss become handmaidens, and these poignant feelings make loving much harder. Only time and a determined effort to continue loving with all of your heart will heal this. The only way to heal this hurt is by loving other people more, especially those who are still with you. The more you love, the more you heal.

Perhaps you may find yourself looking for the meaning of the death of your child. If this thought occurs, it might be a good time to realize that children often come for a short time to assist in spiritually awakening the parent to the many lessons of love. You may or may not be able to embrace this concept. If you can embrace it, you may find that your spiritual awakening really accelerates.

As the grieving parent, allow people to help you. Allow other people to grieve your child along with you. If you help each other, healing can take place much more gently and possibly with greater ease.

How to Help a Parent Who Has Experienced the Death of a Child

If you are the person helping a grieving parent or family, you will need the tools of tremendous kindness, patience, and wisdom. If you feel that words fail you, then it is just fine. Sometimes, there just aren't enough words to help the feelings of this mom or dad. Your dedication to them will help tremendously over time. Always hug them. Always love them and be available for chats and crying sessions. Everyone gets past tears as long as he or she is afforded patience so that these powerful emotions can be safely released.

Call them. Visit them. Talk to them. Remember the anniversary of the death of this child and, if you can, remember the birthday of this child. Remember both events with a lovely card telling the parents that you are thinking of them on this day. Remember how old the child would have been. This activity is appropriate the first two or three years after the child's passing.

Help them with their remaining children if you can. Take them out to lunch, to the movies, to a sporting event, or just to shop. Be a friend.

Ask them to help you with your grief. If you were close to the child, tell them how you are feeling. Some friends and family members may find that they put on a brave face, a face of strength during the day, and just go to pieces themselves at night. Some loving souls just wake up crying.

Remember that you are mourning not just the person who died but the grief that the remaining family members are feeling. Sometimes the feelings are so strong that you do not know whom to grieve first. You have to be patient with yourself. On some really difficult days, it is an interesting experience to call the family and to tell them how much you are grieving them and the child. Ask them for help. This will help them come out of themselves. Your service to these grieving people will be the compassion you would have wanted for yourself.

Finally, be sensitive to the times when the family just wants to be alone. Ask for spiritual guidance, and your service will be that much more powerful and healing.

Death of a Spouse

When a spouse dies, there are so many feelings. Perhaps the first one is of abandonment. *What am I to do now? How do I go on without her? Why did she leave me at this time? We had so much to do! How could he leave me when I need him the most right now?* There is an emptiness that comes with any death. There is a need, almost a demand, to understand why this has happened.

Life on Earth is often looked at as a spiritual schoolhouse, one in which you can have all types of lessons and experiences. The death of a spouse will offer a whole new set of experiences. As this "earthly school" continues, the remaining spouse is now given the opportunity to learn all kinds of new things, to change the course of his or her life, and to understand a new facet of this ever-changing journey on the Earth plane.

If You Are the One Who Is Grieving a Spouse

Love the spouse who left. Never stop loving the life you had together; the life you had hoped would be longer. Love the life you still have left to live without him or her. Live and love with more passion and more commitment. Know that your spouse did not leave to punish you—only to give you the opportunity to learn and to grow in different ways. Your spouse is also going through a unique experience—the experience of death. He or she has to learn to let go and to continue to love. Both parties are grieving, and both parties are having an experience so that a tremendous amount of information can be learned about living and dying. Remember that his or her death is not a punishment, although, considering what you are going through, it may feel as though it is. All of these initial crazy days will pass. You will find yourself returning to a new routine. You will be charting a new course for your life. This is not the course you thought you would have. It is a new course; one that will take you in what may seem like a whole new direction. This direction may open up totally new doors. Some people learn more about themselves after the death of a spouse than they ever thought possible.

Learning how courageous you are is one of the more powerful things a person can discover. While adrenalin carries you through the first difficult days and weeks, it is old-fashioned courage that takes you through the following years without that spouse.

If you have children, one of the hardest things is to handle your own grief and pain while helping them with theirs. Oftentimes, you do not know whom to grieve more—your spouse for leaving or your children for the pain they are enduring. Everyone is going to be turning to you for help and comfort. Your heart is breaking, and you may feel as if you are drowning in the sorrow of this tremendous event.

You may find yourself very angry at this spouse for leaving you with bills to pay, overwhelming debt, and possibly no life insurance. The financial concerns may be almost more overwhelming than the death itself. This level of anger will take time and patience to work through. Whatever the reason was that this spouse left you with this tremendous burden will not be known for quite some time. However, if you are able to work toward finding an answer, you will heal faster.

Take some time and create something that honors the time that you had together. Plant a tree or a garden. Create a piece of art. Create a memory box of treasured moments and include photos, notes, cards, and thoughts about this person. This activity helps to distract children during those early days of grieving and gives them something constructive to do. Do not close your heart. Expand your capacity to love, whether or not it is for your children, for your family, or for his or her family and friends. This action will help you greatly to heal more quickly. Invite people to talk about your spouse; let him or her continue to live in everyone's hearts.

Think back to all the kind and wonderful things you said to this person. Feel the warmth of those words. If the last words you said or the words exchanged between you were not kind and warm, do not despair. Tell him or her now what you wish you could have said then. Invite your children to talk to you about how they are feeling and what they wish they had said. Encourage them to just say those words to the person who has died in the form of a loving prayer.

Remember that love never dies. Love continues for eternity. Even though you will have to move forward with your life without this loved one, you can always send to this soul your love. Even if you choose eventually to remarry, you do not have to cease loving one person to love another. Love that lives within you can expand to embrace everyone in your life now and in the future.

How do you move forward without this person? Each day offers a new opportunity to heal. Each day you can get up, and, if the feeling comes over you, you can cry. Then dry those tears; smile because you had that love, and look forward to a good day.

If people invite you out to enjoy an evening, do it. Begin to be with people as soon as you are able. The longer you shut yourself off from others, the harder it will be to re-enter that emotional place of normal day-to-day relationships with friends and family.

Moving forward does not mean forgetting the spouse who has died. Moving forward does not mean that you are betraying the memory of your spouse. Moving forward means that you are still alive. Moving forward means that you are living and healing.

Sometimes you are going to feel fragile. Everyone feels fragile after a death and after being traumatized by the entire event. However, you can translate that fragile feeling into a growing sense of strength.

Love offers us many lessons. Sometimes you have to learn how to live when someone dies. Perhaps your next life with that person will be a longer one. For now, live each day with patience. You will need patience with yourself and with those around you who do not understand what you are feeling. Allow the future to unfold in its own time.

How to Help When a Spouse Dies

If you are the person helping someone who has lost a spouse, you may find that, as in any death, you are occasionally at a loss for words. In these situations, just offer to listen. Invite the friend or family member out for coffee or a meal and just listen. Let the person cry. Be a true friend. Be patient. Hold and hug the person. Do not be embarrassed by the person's tears. These tears are what will eventually contribute to the person's healing. Spending the energy on tears in the early days allows the emotion to be expressed in a healthy manner. If you let your friend cry on your shoulder, this kindness will help the person to heal faster.

Call the person every day or so. If he or she is not a person with a lot of friends, then give him or her some extra attention. Do not say that this person has to "get on with his or her life and get over this," for this will come across as callous. Do not immediately set the person up with dates. Allow time to heal. Include him or her in gatherings with other friends. Stay by this person's side. Sense when the person is tired and let the person leave early if that is what he or she needs. Grief is exhausting. The fact that he or she participates is courageous enough.

Go to the movies, go shopping, or go to a sporting event. Be available for the person who is grieving. Understand that your help may seem insignificant in the face of his or her loss, but kindness is always significant. Always be kind.

Death of a Parent

When a parent dies before a child reaches roughly the age of twenty-five or so, there can be a profound and persistent feeling of abandonment. There is the feeling that the parent left almost deliberately, as if it were the child's fault, and combined with the emptiness is a feeling of anger and resentment. Often the person just does not know how to express these feelings. The person's life has changed forever, and that directionless feeling is almost overwhelming. The remaining parent and siblings may also be reeling at such a level that each of them feels lost. There doesn't seem to be anyone who can help them all with their pain.

Often the person feels punished by the parent, maybe even unloved. The resentment of "if you really loved me, you wouldn't have left me so suddenly" is hard to remove. Sometimes this resentment sticks like tar to the person and he or she cannot shake it. This can then create the template for misshapen relationships with other people due to feelings of unworthiness of another's love. It can also create the fearful expectation that if you love someone, this person can easily leave you. However, if the parent was very demonstrative and gave much love to the child, the child may have received enough of this love and may never have these feelings. Either way, healing must begin at some point, and such people may feel that they are basically rebalancing their souls.

The children left behind may have such a longing for their parent that it is often hard for them to verbalize it. They imagine what their life would have been like if this parent had lived and had been there for them. They envision how proud this parent would have been, or how much they would have enjoyed watching their life unfold. They miss the feeling of parental approval. They just feel abandoned, as if the death of their parent means that the parent loved them less. This deceased parent will never see their grandchildren and will never be able to offer advice and counsel. Some people continually look for a replacement parent—a father or mother figure.

Grieving the Loss of a Parent

If your parent dies and you are a young person, it is very important to understand that this parent did not deliberately abandon you. Even if the circumstances of the parent's death are questionable, the parent may simply have been so tortured that he or she felt that there was no other way out. No matter how or why a parent dies, the best way to heal your grief is through forgiveness.

Go ahead and be angry with the parent for leaving. Your anger is a facet of your love for this person. You are naturally angry that you cannot spend more time with your parent. Sometimes those hot tears, which well up, need to be allowed to spill out. Anger, frustration, and even rage are normal feelings toward a parent who has left. Eventually, if you allow these emotions to be spent, the anger leaves, the frustration lessens, and the rage melts away into the memories of this parent you loved so much.

If the death of your parent was by illness or accident, it is important to know that while his or her body may not be with you, this parent's love for you did not die. Whether or not your parent is physically present, he or she will always love you.

Find a friend or parent with whom you can vent your feelings. Talking with a sibling can help you both because this is a shared experience. Talk about this parent as much as you want with someone who will encourage you to do so.

While the memories are still fresh in your mind, write down what you want to remember, all the things that you learned, and what you loved most about this parent. Keep this journal by your bed as a comfort. Write to the parent if you feel the need. This also helps you to process your emotions.

Holidays are always hard after any death. Continue to celebrate the holiday, even though you are feeling sad. Continuing to live is the process of healing. Encourage the rest of the family to make the holiday special. The first time will be hard. Each successive year it will be a bit easier. This includes birthdays. If you no longer celebrate that parent's birthday, then perhaps you can take a moment within yourself to remember them in your own way on that day.

Life will never be the same without this parent. It isn't supposed to be the same. The finality of the event will cause every family member's life to be different. How each person adjusts to the change will chart the course for the rest of that person's life. You can choose to be happy and to heal your pain, or you can choose to be miserable and sacrifice yourself because of this death by denying yourself any future happiness. It is unlikely that this parent would want you to be miserable because of his or her passing. Most parents would want you to heal and to continue to live and build on this experience for a powerful, wonderful, meaningful life.

Helping a Child to Grieve a Parent

Helping a child, teen, or young adult will require much patience and tremendous amounts of love. You cannot replace this parent, but you can be there for the grieving person. You can offer to be a true friend and to provide wise counsel. Biology does not always make a family; often, family friends can play a tremendous role in helping a single parent family to heal after a death or a divorce.

Being a friend to a person like this can be especially important. While you are not responsible for the person's healing specifically, you can make a compassionate contribution to this person's insight just by listening and offering encouraging comments. Imagine what you would want someone to say to you if it were you in this situation. Remind your friend that even though his or her parent is not physically here, the parent's love never ceases. Explain that love goes on for eternity like a warm blanket, always warm and comforting. Unlike exhaustible physical bodies, love never, ever dies. Love, which is always present, is never diminished by time or space. Acceptance of the parent's eternal love will help the child to heal. The love is always there.

Buy a log book and help this person write down all that he or she remembers about this parent—the good, the bad, the lessons, the memories, the funny things, and the not-so-funny things. Perhaps create a memory box to help the person organize his or her thoughts and feelings especially about the parent's humanness. Human beings are so complicated that it is more realistic to write down all the things about the parent that need remembering than to expect your mind to remember them forever. Just because someone dies does not mean that he or she immediately becomes a saint. Death does not change someone's personality. If the parent had some bad personality traits, then it is important to learn from them. Help this person to learn all he or she can from this parent's death.

Sometimes this child or young adult or even an adult may ask really hard questions of you, questions for which you may not have the answer. Tell the person that you do not have all the answers. However, by discussing the event and how it has changed everyone, perhaps both of you can come to some precious conclusions. This genuine honesty will enable the person to feel freer to continue the journey of learning. The death of anyone you love forces you to embark on a powerful journey of learning, and the more you embrace that journey, the more completely you heal.

Death of a Friend

When a friend dies, you are immediately struck by the fragile nature of life. You may find that you are prone to introspection and may become depressed. You grieve but are not sure how to grieve your friend. Perhaps the best method is to allow yourself time to mourn and know that this is a normal feeling—one that has to have its own time to process.

Follow all the processes for anyone who has experienced the touch of death, and allow yourself to heal. Do not enter the guilt room of "if only." You had the time you had with your friend, and perhaps that was how it was meant to be. Celebrate your friendship and remember how much this person meant to you. Also realize that there is always the possibility that you may have many more lives with this soul, depending on how the karmic wheel turns and the lessons you both have to learn.

You may also wonder what to say to a family member and how to react. Offer to help in any way you can. Visit the person and help by offering to talk about the person who has left. Some people will welcome this opportunity, and others will find it too painful. Be sensitive to the wishes of the family. Sometimes your friendship of just being there, of calling the person, and of being a true friend, even in this circumstance, is the ultimate service.

Helping Someone Else to Grieve His or Her Friend

Sometimes you may be in a position to help someone else grieve. This may seem challenging, because you may not always know what to say. However, it is always appropriate to just tell the person that you just do not always have all the answers about a death—why someone leaves or why someone dies the way that he or she did. Sometimes all you can do is let the person talk or cry and hold him or her. Help this person to remember all the facets of the one who has died. Help the person to stop feeling any guilt if that is the person's current state. You will never fully understand how your friendship will help because it is different for each person, but the energy of your positive intention will be tremendous.

If you feel it is appropriate, do something that honors this person's friend. This can be to plant a tree in the loved one's honor or give your friend a living plant that will also honor the continuation of life. You can encourage your friend to write a letter telling family members how their loved one touched their (your friend's) life and was helpful. If your friend is a poet, encourage him or her to write a poem about the one who has departed. If your friend is an artist, encourage him or her to create a beautiful card, sculpture, or painting. You can also encourage your friend to do something in the loved one's name, such as donating to the departed friend's favorite charity or life focus. It may surprise you to learn the power of these acts. These gentle acts of kindness soften the pain people are feeling. Your action creates a shared experience. Helping your friend to honor his or her departed friend is a very powerful thing to do.

Love your friend. Remember this person and smile when you think of him or her. These acts will empower him or her to heal. Love and time eventually heal all things.

Death by Suicide

Many people commit suicide seemingly for a variety of reasons. However, the underlying cause is ultimately profound hopelessness. Whether the person is consciously aware of it or not, hopelessness means that person does not see a way out of the darkness that surrounds them. When people lose hope, this sense of hopelessness permeates their very core. In these instances, darkness literally covers them. It is as if all the color of the life force itself, the vibrancy of life, has left their soul, and the darkness saturates their very being. Some of them literally see the world as grey, as if the color of life itself has disappeared.

The energy of this darkness creates the energetic opportunity for a death gate where one did not specifically exist. The blackness of a person's hopelessness blinds him or her to the solution out of this darkness. Often a person cannot hear friends and family trying to help. Often this darkness defines the person's depression.

Suicide is a conscious decision to end life. For whatever reason, people wrongly believe that they will be free of the darkness that pervades them if they physically die. However, once that person has left the body, the person finds that he or she is still in this terrible darkness. Often the darkness is worse on the "other side." Routinely, people who commit suicide are profoundly sorry once they realize that the relief they so desperately sought has not been reached. The reason for this is that a person who can commit such a violent act must be resonating at an extremely low level. Hate, fear, and hopelessness are profoundly low resonance or emotional levels. Violence committed against oneself is the lowest level of all. Unfortunately, when people reach this low level, it dictates their resonance and pulls them into a greater level of darkness. The pain that haunted them in life will continue to haunt them in death.

Many people are adept at hiding this suicidal darkness from family and friends. If a surviving family member never saw the suicide act coming, it may simply be that the soul who left did not want anyone to know how he or she felt. It is extremely important to understand this. Dark feelings frequently exist in an almost "secret life" inside a person. This is where the "trapped," hopeless feelings originate. Perhaps understanding this fact will enable a grieving friend or family member to understand in some way what this person was thinking and feeling and that there is no "fault or blame" to be had by family and friends.

Helping Yourself to Heal the Grief of a Suicide

If you are grieving a loved one due to suicide, there may be emotions attendant with this death that you would not have had if your loved one had died in a different way. You may feel shame at the stigma of suicide and guilt because you may believe that you could have done something to prevent your loved one's suicide. Sometimes a family member's intervention could have made a difference—sometimes not. At the point of death there is no way of knowing what, or if anything, could have helped this person. Often people keep their desire to commit suicide a secret. Some are more vocal. Frequently, families cannot conceive of that level of sadness and do not recognize the cries for help if any were even made.

You have to allow yourself to grieve their loss and their method of death. You may be concerned about what happens to them after death. In this case, it is wise to use the power of prayer to help them wherever they are. Life continues after physical death. You may grieve what may seem like a lost opportunity to stop the event. Some events were just meant to happen, and sometimes there was nothing more anyone could have done to have changed the outcome.

Often, there is a sense of shame at the method of death, especially if your faith labels this method of death a sin. Don't let the method of death define how your family feels about itself for the rest of everyone's life. The person who died had a deep, profoundly personal sadness, which the family very probably would not have been able to alleviate. Families need to have compassion for the person who has left, as well as for themselves. Let this compassion be the defining element for the family—not the artificially applied stigma of suicide.

Release the concepts of sin with this type of death and replace them purely with all the compassion you can bring forth for this person's sadness and personal torture. Even though you may not be able to imagine this level of torture, what matters is that you still love this person. Do not be ashamed at the pain of another. In the end it is not about you; it is about the other person's pain. Sometimes there is such density to the person's pain that no one can relieve it. There is no shame as a surviving family member in accepting this. At this point, you have to accept what you cannot change and use this understanding to help your other family members.

You may feel rage that the person's death has so dramatically changed your life and that you cannot shake this feeling of sadness. Go ahead and vent your anger with someone who is professionally trained to handle this. Under no circumstances keep this anger bottled up inside of you. Do not deny what you feel. Allow these powerful feelings to be expressed in a healthy, balanced way.

Allow yourself time to heal. Understand that people you encounter may not know how to react to your grief. You may end up educating them in the process. This is healing for you, as well as educational for the other person. Do not be afraid to talk about it. It happened. It is a fact, and the more the information is brought out in the open, the faster all the parties can heal.

Helping Someone to Grieve a Suicide

Some people believe that suicide is a terrible sin, a wrong done to themselves and others. There is an artificial stigma attached to this act. Many families feel so ashamed that a family member has died in this manner that their grief is much greater, a torture of "if only" and "what if." All parties in a suicide situation require help—both the living and the soul on the other side. You may be the person helping surviving family members to heal, and you will need to find within yourself tremendous compassion for yourself, as well as for the family members, to work through the painful array of emotions. Remove judgment from the event, especially the concepts of sin. Replace any concept of whether or not this act was a sin with heartfelt compassion for all the parties. Judging is not yours to do. Decide to help the family by just loving them and being there for them.

Allow family members to vent their feelings. Never judge what they say, especially when they are angry at their loved one for leaving them in this way. Encourage them to cry or write about their powerful emotions. Suicide is a life-changing event for all of the relatives left behind. It often feels to them as though life has dealt them a very cruel hand. Eventually, you may be able to point out that this experience—and that is really what it is—will in the end enable them to grow and will also enable them to help other families should this type of death come to their lives.

Love and compassion heal. Let these be your most powerful tools.

Helping a Soul on the Other Side Who Has Committed Suicide

The most powerful way to assist someone who has committed suicide is to send him or her your most profound and compassionate prayers for as long as you possibly can. Prayers light the way and transcend this reality to the "other side" where your loved one is in darkness. The energy of that soul can be lifted up by the hope and love of friends and family. You can ask all of your friends and family members to pray that their loved one be surrounded and helped by angelic beings of light. You can say the 23rd Psalm repeatedly at night before you go to sleep as a gentle spiritual practice to guide this soul to the light of God. Remind this sad soul that God will always love and heal him or her.

You can specifically ask for angels of transition to help the loved one make that essential crossover. With this help, this profoundly depressed soul can find his or her way out of this darkness. No matter what spiritual dimension a soul is in, it is going to take work to heal depression and self–hate. Love the person more, not less, in these challenging times. Long after the death continue to send the person prayers for his or her healing. As you help others to heal, so are you also healed. As you help this soul to heal, you will find that the precious connection to God will also help your own aching heart.

Family Dynamics After a Suicide

The point to be made, regarding suicide, is that sadness, a profound desire to escape the physical body, means you have a choice of what to do. It also means that you have an opportunity to ask for help with the situation and seek a teacher who can help you find meaning in your darkest time. It also means that if one family member commits suicide, other family members, especially young people, will often contemplate it. This is a time to bring in professional help with grief counseling, both in learning how to deal with people outside the family who may not understand and helping individual family members to heal. Healing in this situation will require a unique blend of vigilance, kindness, and patience.

Healing After Suicide

Are people horribly punished for suicide? No, actually they are not. A person who could not bear the pain is not punished as you might think. Many past life regressions show people committing suicide and coming right back to live new lives, to experience new opportunities, and to know love. While karma is created with each type of death, the reality is that we all choose to die of something. We all return to the heaven world at some point. We choose. The dynamics of death are the details that create the karma we will live, life after life. The help you provide another soul even after death can make a tremendous difference to any soul in the process of moving through his or her sojourn in the afterlife.

Multiple Deaths

There are those incredible situations in which you and your family may lose many people all at once, such as in a plane crash, a house fire, or a car accident. Then there are also situations, such as that of the lady who had eight family members die within six weeks of each other, ironically all of different, unrelated causes. She described how overwhelmed and completely numb she felt. She had no idea whom to grieve first or how to begin to handle the settlements of all eight estates, since she was the last living relative. She had to arrange eight funerals. When she related the story, she said that she really had no idea how to begin to sort it all out. She didn't think her body could hold that many tears. Eventually, she spent so much time and money working on the settlement of each estate that she lost her job and her home and had to move in with friends until she could sort everything out. Part of her profound sadness was her aloneness, for the very people she would have gone to for comfort had just died. This wasn't even someone's worst nightmare, because no one could have ever imagined such a bizarre scenario.

In another instance, a family of six was vacationing when their minivan jumped a bridge abutment to avoid an accident and all six family members died. In this case, the remaining family members on both sides of the couple's family had to work together to decide how to handle all the details, from funerals to disposal of that estate. Eventually, they got to the part where they could allow themselves to grieve.

There is the other horrific scenario in which your relative not only kills himself or herself, but he or she also kills other people in the process of committing suicide. For the relatives left behind, there is a horror factor that will affect them in a way that nothing else can. For these people, they will not only grieve the loss of their relative and the people their relative killed, but they will also have to grieve the loss of their family name and reputation—their very identity—seemingly soiled forever by the actions of this family member. It is understood that in a death, your life will be changed, but in this scenario, which is now happening all too frequently, you will see your life so shattered that picking up the pieces will be the challenge of a lifetime. There is also now a chilling isolation as friends and possibly many family members avoid you, believing that somehow what has happened is inherently your fault.

Astounding things happen to people, and that includes the unimaginable loss of multiple people. The logistics of multiple deaths come as a tremendous shock. You have the shock of the deaths themselves, multiple funerals, and often the settlement of multiple estates. You may have to deal with police and criminal investigations. The press may be involved. Grieving often has to take a back seat to the urgency of the immediate actions. Eventually, though, you have to get to the business of grieving each person, and that is a profoundly unique challenge.

If You Are Grieving the Loss of Multiple Family Members

Whom do you grieve first? The enormity of the situation overwhelms you, and you simply do not know where to begin or how to wrap your brain around the loss of so many people. You find that you are also grieving for the surviving family members. You are grieving for so many people for so many reasons that a tidal wave feeling of emotional chaos may envelope you. People have great difficulty recovering from such catastrophic losses. One of the primary things to do is to begin to sort out your feelings. Perhaps you are feeling really badly for yourself. Perhaps you have lost your entire family. Perhaps you have to go to live with a relative. The most chilling element is that the very people you would have gone to for strength, guidance, and comfort in this situation may be the very people who have just died. If several children have died, the magnitude of the situation is utterly shattering. This alone is a tremendous amount to grieve. What can you do to begin to heal this?

The first step is to be as patient as possible with yourself. Everything will take longer than you expect. This level of grieving and just living day-to-day will take every single ounce of courage and energy you ever thought you could possibly have.

Grieving is exceptionally tiring, but grieving multiple deaths is beyond exhausting. You will have to give yourself extra time to rest. You may find that you have to limit your activities until you can begin to return to some sense of balance. Be sure to take vitamin supplements to keep up your strength. Eat, even though food may have lost its taste for you.

Ask your employer, family, and friends to help you, and then give them specific things to do. If you don't know what you need them to do, brainstorm with them and then begin to delegate tasks so that all that has to be done can be done.

Ask your employer if you can work half days for awhile and explain that you are seeking to regain your balance and part of that is managing your tremendous fatigue level. Keep your employer updated on what is happening in your situation. Eventually, things do begin to calm down. Keeping key people informed will help them to support you more. You may have to take a leave of absence to handle all the details of all of these deaths.

When you love, you have the ability to love many people at the same time because love is virtually effortless in its energy expenditure. However, grieving requires that you focus on grieving one person at a time when at all possible, because grieving takes tremendous amounts of energy. If you are able to do this, begin to separate your grief. Grieve one person for an entire week. This means to focus on who this person was to you, how much you loved him or her, and how much you will miss this loved one. Write down your feelings about this person. Write the person a letter or record in a diary all that you are experiencing. Talk about it with other friends or family members who are willing to help and to listen. Each week rotate whom you will grieve. In this way you can give an equal amount to each soul who died.

As you do these activities, you may find that you are grieving one person more than another. This may be because you had a unique place for this person in your heart. This could also be for many other reasons, including the possibility that this particular person's death left many things unresolved. Now you have no way to settle them with that person. Whatever the reason was for this happening, you will have to resolve it within yourself. Work on the forgiveness process. This may mean seeking to learn the lessons that person taught you. In this way you will learn to hold those experiences as exceptionally valuable, even if they were emotionally difficult.

If you are feeling guilt or shame, remorse or anger, figure out whether these feelings are actually warranted or whether you think this is how you are *supposed to feel*. Sometimes you may have a preconceived idea of what is expected of you. You feel what you feel, and you grieve in the method that enables you to heal. Each person's grief is unique. Allow yourself to grieve in your own way.

No matter what has happened, it is wise to remember that guilt and shame are extremely toxic, physically and emotionally, and can stop the healing process. Do not give in to the emotional trap of "what if" and "if only." Whatever took place before these deaths is over. The time has come to decide to heal. This will take unparalleled courage. Asking for spiritual guidance will be especially important at this time. Pray, asking God to help you find your way out of this sad time.

Gradually, over time, a growing level of peace will come to you. How long that takes is in direct proportion to the amount of actual grief work you do. When grief waves hit you, go ahead and cry. If you are not comfortable crying in public, excuse yourself to a restroom and let those tears go. Do not stop your tears. You will get to the other side of them, and every tear shed helps to wash the grieving heart and bring in new hope.

In this situation tremendous patience is required to work through this level of grief, and it is often difficult work just to get through each day. Great compassion is required in this situation—for yourself and every person associated with the event. Grief counseling would be of tremendous benefit here.

If You Are Helping Someone Grieve the Loss of Multiple Family Members

If you are helping someone who has suffered such a catastrophic loss, one of your greatest levels of service will be simply to listen to the person talk about each loved one and the dynamic logistics of what they are experiencing. Your patience is critical for this person's healing. In this way, you may find that both of you heal.

Help out with mundane things like grocery shopping, house cleaning, walking the dog, or watching children. If the weight of the grief in the house becomes too much for you, take some time for yourself and then return to help.

Grief at this level is beyond anyone's normal sense of comprehension. You may find that you are utterly exhausted. Do not deny this feeling. Often, those seeking to offer help and compassion feel guilty when they experience exhaustion and emotional burnout. This is normal. Stop, rest, and then return to help the grieving person once again. This break is critical to keep you and the other person in some semblance of balance. If several friends are helping, rotate the duties.

One of the most crucial duties may be helping extremely difficult family members or members who have become seriously depressed, profoundly guilty, or utterly despondent. Special care will be required here. Again, someone may have to watch them during this most critical time so that they can get to the other side of this painful experience.

Pray for yourself. Pray for the family. Pray for those who have died. Pray for healing and strength, and absolutely pray for the wisdom to say the right thing at the right moments.

Always remember that, although this level of service is perhaps the most challenging thing you will ever do, it means that you will grow as a person and that you will never be the same.

All events change us. Some change us so completely that no matter what our role in that terrible moment—either as grieving family member or person helping—the goal is to find some level of emotional balance. Finding your emotional and spiritual footing after such staggering losses is critical for the path of soul evolution for all of you. You will never see yourself the same way again. You will never take anything for granted, and one of the most powerful challenges will be learning to regain trust for life itself. You may find that you are angry with God for causing all of your family and friends so much pain, and yet, in that very conversation with God, there is healing.

One of the hardest things is to move forward with your life after such an event. It seems almost inconceivable that you could ever go back to the mundane aspects of living such as doing yard work, going to the movies, or just having a good night's sleep. All the aspects of your life have changed, and that change will take time, patience, and wisdom to fully incorporate into a new life.

How Friends and Relatives Grieve

If you are a friend or relative of the person who has died, you are in a distinctly unique position. Even though the transitioned soul is not your child or parent or sibling, your love for the immediate family may place you in a position to grieve deeply, as well. You may or may not have had a profound relationship with the person who left. Your relationship may be with the parent or sibling. You may experience a series of emotions as you watch people you love go through their grieving process. If your role is to help them, then you have to be able to find a way to release your own feelings of sadness. You may also grieve the feeling that your efforts have only a marginal affect on the situation, but that is not true. No energy is ever wasted, and the love and energy you put into your compassionate efforts to help family and friends are tremendously important.

Your efforts do help. You just have to be patient with the family member and especially with yourself. You have to give yourself time to grieve too. It is important to acknowledge that your grief, while not as supremely exquisite as your immediate family members' hurt, still puts you in a very painful place.

If you were very close to the soul who left, then you have dual levels of grief. You grieve for the soul, because you miss that person, and you grieve for the immediate family. Either way, you have much work ahead of you.

The first time you see or call on the grieving friends or relatives after the death will be hard. Each time you talk to them, you are going to be mindful of their grief. There does come a point when you can tell them that you are grieving, too, and that you need their help. Even though you may not want to "bother them with your stuff," in an ironic way, helping you helps them. It forces them to come out of their pain for a brief moment to help you. They can see how the death of their child, spouse, or sibling has affected others and how your grief is very personal and painful. Knowing that other people cared deeply for their loved one is comforting and healing for them. It also reminds them how their loved one affected so many other lives. No one has a monopoly on grief. It is a unique feeling for all people connected with the event or person.

It is wise to remember that the entire country grieved for the souls lost on September 11, 2001, even if we did not know anyone who died on that day. We all grieved because our world had changed forever. Things have never been quite the same, and they never will be. Through helping each other, we, as a country, began to heal. Compassion and sensitivity to the needs of others allow us to open our hearts to a healing path. Coming out of ourselves focuses our attention on someone else and enables us to rise to a higher calling of service to others, even in subtle moments. Caring for others is the ultimate lesson of love.

Death of a Pet

You love your pets. Pets provide unconditional love. They are always there, and their loyalty is absolute. You live with them for five to twenty years. This amount of time is a major portion of a human life. These animals often pull you out of depression, save your emotional life, and provide unimagined comfort. You cry in their fur and hug them for that poignant physical bond. Pets hear your most intimate thoughts. They kiss you, hug you in their own manner, stay by your side, and sleep with you. You just adore your pets. Their companionship is precious.

If You Are Grieving Your Pet

If you have to have a pet put to sleep, it may be of tremendous comfort to have a close friend go with you. These are often agonizing moments as you watch your pet's life slip away. You may not want to drive to the vet or back. It is good to ask for help in these times.

When a pet dies in any manner, you may feel embarrassed that you grieve so deeply, as if the pet's love were any less important than the love of a human person. Animal personalities are just as distinct, just as memorable, and just as important to grieve as the personality of a human being because animals provide so much love.

Grieve for your animal. Find someone else who has also known the loss of a pet and just talk about what you love and remember about your pet. There is no shame in loving an animal or grieving his or her death. It is always important to honor a creature that loved you dearly. Your pets love you in good times and in bad and through all the experiences you have. Pets also live through all of your experiences with you.

The grief waves come to you just as surely with an animal's passing as they do with a person's. Allow them to come. Honor the pet, and remember that this pet will be there to meet you when it is your turn to transition into the heaven world.

Something that often happens after the death of a pet is that the owner is too grief-stricken to get another pet. This is unfortunate, because the owner still has so much love to give. Grieve for as long as you need to, and then, if it is feasible, get another pet. Getting another pet will not dishonor the memory of the wonderful creature who has just died; in fact, it will be testimony to the love you have to give to all animals.

If You Are Helping Someone to Grieve a Pet

Many people feel that it is not okay to grieve their pet. A number of people say that it was "just an animal." It is actually important for anyone who has deeply loved an animal to honor this pet with his or her grief. One of your most important jobs will be to help that person to grieve the pet. Tell the former owner that it is not just okay to mourn the creature, but it is important. Let the owner cry about it. Offer to help, or see how they are doing over time, because their tears will come more than once. You can be sure that this gentle service will long be appreciated.

10

WHAT TO DO FOLLOWING A DEATH

Do not consider so much what others should do for or to
you, *but what will you do for and towards others. And real-*
ize that all of these must be constructive in their nature.
Edgar Cayce Reading 1889-1

The Responsibility of the
Grieving Person or Family

As hard as this may be to believe, the grieving person or family
has a job to do when it comes to communicating with extended
family and friends. This obligation includes divorces or any other
kinds of tragedy including financial disasters. The sad truth about
our society is that no one knows what to say or to do in the event
of a death, a natural disaster or the end of a relationship. When
people see someone grieving, they realize that somehow their
worst fears have come true for someone else. Since they feel they
could not face this situation themselves, they think they cannot
face you either. What do you do?

Find a quiet space inside your heart and decide your course of
action. That course is an honest appraisal of how you, at least,
think you want your life to be after this life crisis. You have to
decide how you want other people to relate to your family, and
you have to tell them how to relate to you specifically. This advice

pertains to any type of death or grief previously discussed. Remember, as you face others and help them heal, so are you healed. This is a very therapeutic action for all parties involved. You may think that you do not want to tell people this information because it feels difficult, but you need to do it to plan for the future you and your family will be living. Giving people direction in how to relate to you, as described below, will help everyone heal faster in the long run.

- Decide that you want people to still call you.
- Ask to be invited out to lunch or supper.
- Have kids over to play.
- Tell people it is okay to wave when they see you.
- Tell them it is okay to talk about their families, kids, spouses, and pets.
- Tell them it is okay to talk about the person who has left, for whatever reason or whatever disaster has befallen you. Tell them you will be all right and that the talk helps you to grieve and to heal.
- Tell them that you may cry sometimes and that their service to you can be a long, gentle hug. They don't have to say anything. Their presence and their courage in helping you is what matters most. They are going through this with you, especially close family members, friends, and neighbors.
- Give them permission to tell you how they are feeling at the change in your life situation, because they are grieving, too. This acknowledgment will bring you out of yourself and enable you to help them much more. You will be healed, as well.
- Gratitude expressed specifically is tremendously healing, especially when thank you notes are sent to the people who helped you the most, or when you make a cake or cookies for neighbors who really went that extra mile.
- If emergency services were involved, go to the police precinct, EMS station, hospital, or other agency that helped you and tell them thank you. This forces you out of yourself and enables you to think of others. This helps you to rise above pain.
- Decide that you will eventually be all right, that you will be able to chart a new path, and that this path will include all these wonderful people who are still in your life.

• Decide that when people do ask you to go out or to do something with them, you will go no matter how you are feeling. This is a commitment not only to yourself but also to the person who asked you. Many times it takes quite a bit of courage for a friend to ask you out. Reward the friend by going. It will teach that person how to help others in your situation.

• Decide in advance to forgive people for the often thoughtless things they may say when they think they are trying to help you with your grief, or they don't know what to say.

• Decide that you are healing, and thank everyone for helping you.

Disposition of a Body

If money were no object, then what would be the best way to handle a body at death? Perhaps the best method has been and continues to be cremation because of the concept of attachment. Once a body is not physically here, then attachment can begin to cease. This is enormously helpful to the soul who has transitioned to the heaven world. This is truly an occasion when you must think not just about yourself and your family but also about the soul who has left. Honor the loved one's wishes if that person requested burial, but also remember the importance of ceasing attachment.

Many people want a grave to visit, believing that their loved one is there, but no soul on a spiritual path stays in a graveyard. Once in the heaven world, the soul travels through all the schools of the heaven worlds. The soul can be reached through prayer and positive thought. Visiting a grave, although a physical symbol, prolongs attachment to a person who is not there and, in a very subtle way, retards the progress of the soul in the heaven world and the progress of the grieving person.

Cremation is kinder to the Earth. The burial of a physical body is a burden on the Earth because the decomposition process takes a very long time and releases toxic substances in that process. It is easier to loosen attachments through the process of releasing the energy of the body through the fires of purification.

Perhaps consideration should be given to having a modest memorial service for family and friends and then a very small service for immediate family with the body or at the gravesite.

What do you do with the ashes? You should return them to the Earth or take them to the sea and spread them across the waves. The point is to complete the cycle of healing by returning the energy of a physical body to the Earth. Keeping ashes forever is another method of attachment. Keep them for awhile if you must, but just as you must let go of the soul, you must also release the ashes, as well. Eventually, you will know when the time is right.

Family Dynamics and Difficult Personalities

Times of crisis do not always bring out the best in people. When someone close to you dies, you might expect that everyone, all friends and family members, would be at their compassionate best. Unfortunately, this does not always happen. Disagreements can erupt very easily over everything from the day of the funeral to the method of disposal of the body as well as funeral arrangements, the choice of a funeral home, music selections, flowers, invitations, and ensuing ceremonies—not to mention the disposition of the estate.

Tensions rise when family members come to the house of the person who has died. This means that grieving family members are essentially entertaining other family members, providing everything from sleeping accommodations to meals and transportation. People who are raw with grief should never have to entertain after a death. If they want one person to act as a coordinator to help with phone calls, greet guests, and manage arrangements, then that is the only person who should be staying at the home. Ask everyone else to stay in a hotel. While this may sound harsh, it reduces the strain on the primary grieving family. Thank them for staying in a hotel and for understanding the sensitivity of the situation. This humble gratitude will hopefully mitigate any hurt feelings.

A grieving family must have quiet time alone in their own home simply to mourn, to cry, and to have some privacy. The most intimate moments of grief are extremely personal and just cannot be shared in public. It is hard enough to put on a brave face during the daylight hours days following a sudden death; but it is excruciating to have to continue that act when the day ends.

There is also the problem of people who are negative and who bring difficulties with them upon arrival. If you have someone who is going to do or say anything that will exacerbate the grief of the mourning family, then, as politely as possible, suggest that the family may not be up to having that difficult person come at all. People want to keep family peace, but the prime objective is the care of the grieving family. It is *only* about their feelings. It takes a lot of courage to deny a negative person from coming, but at this point, the family simply cannot take on any more pain. If you are the person who must make this decision, keep in mind what is the greatest good for all the parties involved and do not just bow to the wishes of the most difficult or controlling family member, no matter what that person's position in the family may be.

Some people are foul weather friends and family members. They revel in the difficulties of others. They loudly and piously ask what they deem to be "helpful questions." People try to be polite, hoping that the awkwardness will subside, but that negative person can poison a situation when a family is trying to begin the healing process. Frequently, family feuds break out at a funeral. This unpleasantness is unnecessary. If you have to help plan the funeral, give some consideration to whether or not certain relatives are going to be there for the benefit of all concerned. If they are not, then do not have them come. Remember: Allowing a toxic person to attend a funeral will not only not keep peace but can also cause the primary family greater hurt. With the toxic family members present at the funeral, there will be no peace. Take a stand and protect the family. Remember not to be afraid to ask that people stay in hotels, and remember that you are not required to entertain people. Feelings are so raw and vulnerable during this time that it will take all of your courage to pick the highest road for all concerned.

Some people love the follow-on drama after a death. It is a good idea to continue to find a way to distance yourself from "helpful" toxic people and relationships. These people keep wounds open and inflict new ones. You would be wise to stay away from them with as much love as you can.

Employer Responsibilities

Ultimately, companies are families. Some are closer than others and some are more sensitive than others. When an employee experiences a death in their family, it can affect many employees. The way in which companies handle an employee's death situation will come back to haunt them or to laud them long after the initial time is over. The US military considers this responsibility such an important job that it always assigns an officer or a senior enlisted person to be a direct liaison with the family to help and support them with every follow-on aspect of the death. This service is long remembered.

To a Grieving Employee

When an employee has a death in the family, often the employer is initially sympathetic. However, the relentless requirements of a person's job may require that the employee return to work immediately. For the most part employers do not want to appear insensitive, but they do have a job to get done, and they are paying that person without receiving benefit. The dollars and cents of the situation make things very awkward. The initial actions of the employer will long be remembered and will not only be watched by the other employees but will also directly affect the morale of your company. This is a time for intense compassion—not just looking at the bottom line.

Following these guidelines may be beneficial to the employee and the employer in assisting someone during a difficult time.

• Call the employee immediately; send a generous bouquet of flowers or a large basket of fruit, and then visit the grieving employee. Don't just ask: "What can I do?" The employee doesn't know how to answer that.

• Immediately give the employee two solid weeks off if the death is a child, a spouse, sibling, or close parent.

• Contribute generously to and take up a collection for funeral expenses. Funerals cost anywhere from $3,000–$15,000.

• Depending on the employee's state of grieving, call the person every week and ask how he or she is. Suggest that the employee return

to work on the third week, only half days, to see how the person does.
•   Offer either to pay for or subsidize grief counseling. This may pay big dividends later. Most grieving people will not pay for or seek grief counseling. Consequently, this will prolong their grief and greatly reduce their productivity for you and emotional healing for themselves. Once serious depression sets in, the work habits of a normally terrific employee may not be what you remembered. Getting mad at a depressed person serves no purpose and makes the employer look like a monster.
•   Once the employee has returned to work, ask the person how he or she is and engage him or her in conversation about the person who has died. Care.
The bottom line for any employer is to give this employee the compassion that you would want for yourself if this were your situation. This compassion will be repaid to you and your company a thousand times.

To a Grieving Family of an Employee Who Dies

When an employee dies, the responsibility of the employer is even greater than that mentioned above. The employee's family will need all the help it can get. Depending on the circumstances of the death, the employer may want to assign someone to the family as liaison to help with everything from understanding employee death benefits to assistance with funeral arrangements.
The employer cannot do too much in this case. The family's whole world has changed forever. Though the employer has lost an employee who is more or less readily replaced, the family has lost its breadwinner, and, if it is a single-parent household, this is a devastating situation for any surviving members. The family will long remember the kindness, generosity, and compassion of your company. Companies are ultimately families of people working together. If this is a large firm, your human relations department head will want to take charge of this matter.
•   If the employee dies on the job, send someone to the house at once to collect the immediate family. If possible, take a clergyman or someone else to help break the news.

- Contribute to and take up a collection for as much cash as possible. The loss of an income producer can be financially catastrophic.
- Assign a liaison person to help with company death benefits if they are due to the family of the deceased.
- Assist the family in providing notice for when the funeral will be.
- Make sure that there is food for the grieving family.
- Offer to assist with funeral arrangements.
- Ensure that family members who need to be contacted have been and that there is someone staying with children if this is a single-parent household.
- If finances will now be a serious problem, consider setting up a college fund for the children for their future.
- If the press is involved, assist the family with maintaining its privacy.
- Hold a company funeral service for employee friends and co-workers of the deceased.
- Hold group grief counseling for employee co-workers who may be suffering grief and shock at this person's sudden death.
- Respect the privacy of the family if it does not accept offers of help.

Death is an opportunity to rise to the occasion with your finest humanity. Death presents an opportunity to be of tremendous service. Death is the time when what you do at that moment will be extremely meaningful. Let the memory of what one company or one person can do echo compassionately for a very long time.

11

JUDGING THE TRAUMATIC EVENT

Keep [your soul] in patience, in love, in gentleness, in kindness . . . for these are indeed the fruits of the spirit . . .
Edgar Cayce Reading 5322-1

The Burden of Judgment

Whenever a death is experienced, one of the initial reactions is to
judge within you, whether this event is good or bad. Because you
feel sadness and pain at any death, you have a tendency to judge
the event as terrible. When someone you love dies, you are in
such tremendous pain that it is impossible at that moment to have
any perspective on the situation. Judging the situation as profoundly tragic automatically leads you down the road of much
pain. Very often, that pain is partnered with a tremendous load of
guilt brought on by the agonies of "what if" and "if only."

If judgment involves a burden of pain and guilt, then the long-
term goal in any situation would be to work through your emotional challenge of grieving and to release pain and guilt and
ultimately judgment. When this burden is released, you can feel a
unique kind of freedom and grow to understand others and yourself better.

The challenge of releasing judgment is allowing the possibility or the concept that everything that happens to a soul—every emotional pain, every joyous event, and every moment of supreme awakening—is for that soul's highest purpose. Judging an event, a death, or even a murder as terrible robs the experience of its highest meaning and its greatest lesson.

We are seldom privy to why things happen. We shake our heads and hope that this "terrible thing" never happens to us. We shudder in horror at what has occurred to another person or to another family. But what if the event is not necessarily terrible in the much larger picture of the long-term cosmic view of life? What if one person's death has helped someone else? What if the death of a six-year-old enables that soul to help other children trying to cross over, because that seeming child was really a much more advanced soul? What if a soul needed only a few precious moments of mortal life to fulfill its life mission and then by its death, offered all the members of a family the opportunity to grow spiritually? Is that death a tragedy, or it is just an opportunity that has not been identified?

Looked at in a mundane, almost abstract way, consider when you go to the grocery store, do you always fill up your cart? Sometimes do you just "run in for a few things?" Do you find that sometimes you get a few extra things, and then you leave, but your cart is still not full? No one would judge this as odd or tragic. You purchased only the things you needed, and then you left. No one would even comment on this. Mortal life is a grocery store of experiences; often we come and shop for only a few things. However, the ramifications of that brief "shopping trip" will echo out through time.

Understanding the events surrounding a death still requires our utmost compassion and our deepest caring. But that same understanding can help us to grow, if—if we can look beyond the emotion of the event and open our spiritual hearts to finding the highest good that can come from anyone's death.

In the 2001 attack on the World Trade Center, many people saw the deaths of all the people and calamity as a horrific event. At this point, no one knows what the long-term story will be and how it will shape our future. We do know that the passengers who died on the American Airlines Flight 93 crash in Pennsylvania did so to save many lives. Is their death a tragedy or a blessing to untold thousands? Perhaps it is both. Sometimes, events can be tragic and essential all at the same time. Is this event the catalyst for something important to come, something that somehow had to get our attention? We truly do not know.

The Civil War is another interesting example of a traumatic event. The United States was less than 100 years old in 1860 when the South seceded from the Union. The 5 years of fighting that encompassed the Civil War left a staggering 860,000 people dead, half the country in ruin, and a mountain of pain, anguish, vengeance, and suffering in its wake. Was this event good or bad? It was both. Because of this terrible war, the United States took a stand against slavery at a huge cost in black and white American lives. Because of this stand, the country rebuilt and became stronger than ever. However, the real test of why the Civil War had to be won by the North became clear very much later in a terrifying way. If the South had been successful in its succession efforts, what country would have had the power, the courage, and the raw strength to fight not just the Kaiser but more specifically Hitler and Hirohito? Who could have kept Stalin in his place and stopped his own goal of world domination, or China's Chairman Mao? Only a young country that had witnessed, first hand, the tragic price of peace could give its heart to helping other countries have their peace maintained.

For this reason, it is wise to observe and to cry, if you must, but to reserve judgment on the most recent terrorist events to hit the United States. These events happened for a reason. All the participants seem to be here, ready to do their part. The stage is set. Although watching it happen is often excruciating, you are wise when you reserve judgment on how the future will unfold.

"God never gives you more than you can handle."

How many times have you heard someone utter this phrase? You are suffering grief or financial troubles or illness or problems with your marriage or relatives or kids, and some well-intentioned person utters this statement. Just exactly what does it mean? Does it mean that if you are struggling with it, you can't handle it? Does it mean that if you long for a simpler solution, you are denying something that God actually said or meant? What about someone who commits suicide? Does this mean that this person is judged to have been unable to handle life itself? What about the man or woman who suffers spousal abuse? Is the abused spouse handling the situation if he or she leaves or stays? Judging someone from this point of view is difficult since you are unable to define "handling something."

Each soul chooses its experiences, which is the basis of *free will*. You have free will so that you can choose how you will respond to various situations in each life you live. In some lives, you have more challenging experiences for the lessons that they offer. Ultimately, you are responsible for what happens in your life. So with personal responsibility as your basic premise, let's say that a soul experienced a terrible parent, who beat and sexually molested him or her. If this person feels like a victim throughout life, is that handling it? Or if he or she fights back, rejects this parent, and learns difficult lessons, is that handling it better?

For example, when a person commits suicide, he or she is often judged as "taking the easy way out." It is possible that you truly do not have all the facts regarding this person's despair, and, therefore, you cannot judge what a person can or cannot "handle."

People frequently say things that they think are helpful at the moment yet are really quite thoughtless. None of us knows the pain of another, especially in a grief situation. How could we? Hence, taking extra care in what you say becomes critically important. Instead of offering a meaningless platitude about what God did or did not intend, try telling the person that you believe him or her to be a really good person and that your heart is with him or her in this difficult time. It is also important not to tell someone that you know just how they feel because you cannot possibly know how someone else feels in any type of grief situation. Offer help, but allow the person to decide how much of it to accept.

"I'll pray for you."

When you are praying for people, you can send the purity of prayer without judgment. Pray that they receive the needed help—not the answer that you think is right; again, prayer can be *extremely* judgmental. If you feel that you must pray for a change to occur within them, pray that they may have the internal fortitude to overcome any karmic weaknesses that they are encountering. Then trust that all will be at peace. Use the power of prayer to pray for the entire world—not just for one person or yourself. Pray for all in the plant and animal kingdom and the Earth. Pray that you may have guidance in handling your own life situations and knowledge in how to assist others while removing all judgment. It is also very powerful to send healing to every grieving person without judgment.

The Healing Path

Healing is a fascinating path. Doesn't everyone want to heal physical ailments as well as grief? Can't everyone be healed? Doesn't everyone ask for healing when he or she is grieving? Sometimes you have to ask for help and healing and feel worthy to receive it. God will not deny you your experiences. It is important that you do not judge the path of another. It is so easy to blame someone else. You are especially likely to blame another when it appears that a person was truly at fault, such as not watching a child in a swimming pool, or when the person who died acted seemingly recklessly. However, it is not up to you to blame anyone else. All that occurs in mortal life happens in perfect harmony with the divine, even when we cannot see it, do not understand it, and have no practical frame of reference for it. Because of this truth, one of the surest roads out of severe grieving is the willingness to release blame. Edgar Cayce described it in this manner:

> But Know that these conditions [death of a child], for all, are to be used in a manner in which there is no resentment, no animosity, no blame. Just know rather that it is; it cannot be changed—in the present—and that the soul has preferred to stay with its Maker.
>
> Then, the anxiety would be rather in that more and more ye can be, ye are—if ye take the associations in such a manner—in a closer walk with Him, who is the Giver of all good and perfect gifts; who taketh life, who giveth life; that is, in

taking life it is God—and that it is withheld, it is in those conditions in which all are so overcome with disappointment, discouragement.

Do not blame anyone. Do not hold any feeling against those who may have or may not have neglected, who may not have carried out that as might have been possible; but know, thy Redeemer liveth—and that flesh of thy flesh is one again with thy Maker. 480-37

Even if people refuse help and stay in the darkness of prolonged grief, it is important to love them anyway. Send them prayers anyway. This is a time for detached compassion. Some individuals feel the need to experience every aspect of their painful grief. It is not up to you to judge this choice in any way. When they are ready, a teacher who is right for them will appear to help them with their healing path. You can trust that this is so, and then move on with your own path.

Things Aren't Always What They Seem

Two traveling angels stopped to spend the night in the home of a wealthy family. The family was rude and refused to let the angels stay in the mansion's guest room. Instead, the angels were given a small space in the cold basement. As they made their bed on the hard floor, the older angel saw a hole in the wall and repaired it. When the younger angel asked why, the older angel replied, "Things aren't always what they seem."

The next night, the pair came to rest at the house of a very poor but very hospitable farmer and his wife. After sharing what little food they had, the couple let the angels sleep in their bed where they could have a good night's rest. When the sun came up the next morning, the angels found the farmer and his wife in tears. Their only cow, whose milk had been their sole income, lay dead in the field. The younger angel was infuriated and accused the older angel, "How could you have let this happen? The first man had everything, yet you helped him. The second family had little but was willing to share everything, and you let the cow die."

"Things are not always what they seem," the older angel replied.

"When we stayed in the basement of the mansion, I noticed there was gold stored in that hole in the wall. Since the owner was so obsessed with greed and unwilling to share his good fortune, I sealed the wall so he wouldn't find it. Then last night as we slept in the farmer's bed, the angel of death came for his wife. I gave him the cow instead. Things aren't always what they seem." (Author unknown)

Sometimes that is exactly what happens when things don't turn out the way you think they should. If you have faith, you just need to trust that every outcome is always for the greater good. You just might not realize this point until sometime later.

Judging the End of Something

When you encounter the end of anything, the natural human tendency is to judge whether this is a good or a bad event. The fact of the matter is that one of the best ways you can help others is to cease all judgment of any situation in which you find yourself. The bottom line is that *everything* that happens to you occurs for the greater good, even when it seems terribly hard. The more you judge the occurrence, the harder it will be to understand that greater good. Ceasing judgment will enable you to see the larger picture of what has happened: how everything fits into the whole of the cosmic view, the long–term view of soul evolution. The wisdom of all aspects of non–judgment will take you a very long way in the process of healing death. It is this wisdom that helps you be of greater service because of your patience and your hope for a positive outcome, regardless of the situation. This concept can work well if you are even slightly detached from the event. You can step back and realize that yes, we can all learn something from this situation, once we dry our tears.

However, when someone you love dies, when the situation is profoundly personal and intimate, you are instantly thrown into an emotional maelstrom. Even if you think you know that everything which happens to you happens for your greater good, right now in this sickening moment this fact is impossible to understand. All you can know is how bad you feel. When a child dies, for example, you know that you don't understand why it happened. Perhaps forty years from now you could say, it wasn't good, it wasn't bad, but today, in this moment, it is just really, really bad.

So how do you, as the person grieving come to terms with acquiring a perspective on the death of a child by drowning, a spouse killed by a drunk driver, a friend who has committed suicide, a relative who murders other people, a sister who was raped and murdered or a house that is destroyed by a tornado in ten seconds? What good can come from any of this? How do you acquire perspective on the unthinkable? How can you possibly cease judgment of these events?

You must first allow yourself time to grieve. You must work through all those waves of emotions that drown you in their intensity. You must allow yourself time to think about the connecting events that are attendant with any death or ending event. When someone dies or you experience a divorce or your home is destroyed, you meet all kinds of people who are getting to know you on the worst day of your life. As you begin to emerge from the fog of shock and grief, you may begin to ask yourself why you met these people. All right, at first you don't care why you met them; but eventually, you, as a mature, thinking person, may just ask that question.

You may allow yourself to step away from the often prison–like qualities of grief, look outside those cold walls, and notice the people who helped you. Think of the compassion of the rescue workers who let you cry on their shoulders. Imagine how hard it was for the police officers who had to tell you the unthinkable. What is it like for them to deal with emotional trauma day after day? Can you conceive of the heartbreak for emergency room personnel who could not resuscitate a child? Many of these good people find that they are all in tears, feeling that somehow they have failed the parents. That child's death will impact them for a long time.

When you have the courage to keep asking the question of why you met these people and why you had this experience, you notice that other people have put aside their own challenging days and have stepped up to help you with yours. Perhaps something you said or did actually helped them. As you learn how to face that shadow self that is grief and slowly show that unwanted self out the door, you can come to the realization that you are a much wiser person because of this death, divorce, or disaster. Eventually, the prison walls of mourning that have closed you off from the world begin to melt away and you can see the rest of the world again.

Your heart is more compassionate; your joy in things is greater, and your desire to be a caring person to others is larger. Your personal changes may help other people. Slowly, with the gentlest mercy you can show yourself, you can come to appreciate that this initially staggering experience may have been for your most profound growth. This insight will be hard won, and the acquisition of this insight does not mean that you are glad for the event because that thought would engender guilt. You are grateful to have learned from the experience. You are slowly but surely detaching from the emotion and embracing the experience for all the learning it is offering you. The more you learn, the more you evolve.

The more evolved you become as a soul, the more service you can provide. That may have been the very reason for the event after all, no matter how sad that event initially appeared. And yes, there may very well come a day when you can actually say that the event was not good or bad, it was just a learning experience. You may even rise to the level of being grateful to all the players in the event for the lessons they gave you, for truly these lessons were hard won. Perhaps you wrote a book, taught a class, changed the way the world does business, or were just a more helpful neighbor. Whatever you did, however you applied the knowledge of this event was the purpose of the event; for without it, you could not possibly be the person you are today. This is why eventually ceasing judgment of the event will take you a very long way down your healing road.

Judging Death

People judge a person at death. You judge yourself at the death of another, wondering if you loved them enough, often harshly judging yourself in the process.

> Yet in the end. . . When one has put away all the books, and all the words; when one is alone with oneself, when one is alone with God; what is left in one's heart? Just this: I wish we had loved Johnny more . . . Of course we loved Johnny very much . . . Loving Johnny more. What does it mean? What can it mean now? All parents who have lost a child will feel what I mean. Parents all over the earth who lost sons in the war have felt this kind of question and sought an answer. To me, it means loving life more, being more aware of life, of one's fellow human beings, of the earth. It means obliterating, in a curious but real way, the ideas of evil and hate and the enemy; and transmuting them, with the alchemy of suffering, into ideas of clarity and charity. It means caring more and more about other people, at home and abroad, all over the earth. It means caring more about God."[9]

This is the opportunity to cease judgment of all aspects of death. It is not good or bad; it just is. It is an end and a beginning. It is change. Change is the only constant you know—change into seeing the experience of death as an opportunity to learn the lessons of living, no matter how painful.

Judging Suicide

Suicide is judged almost universally. You work overtime to stop other people from committing suicide. Is this right? If you talk someone out of killing himself, the perception is that you have done the right thing. Perhaps all you have done is stop an action for the moment. The reason for the person's profound despair is not necessarily solved. You feel triumphant that you talked someone out of jumping off a bridge or using a gun. While important and another opportunity for the soul, it is, in the large scheme of things, frequently only a momentary reprieve. It is up to the soul to recognize that this momentary reprieve may change the rest of this and future lives. Hopefully, the person will see it that way. But what if he or she doesn't? What if this person persists in his or her desire to leave?

If the soul wants to leave, for whatever the reason, then the soul will leave. Sometimes souls cannot find enough love. Sometimes they remember what the heaven world feels like, and the longing to return to this unforgettable feeling is overwhelming. Sometimes the soul thought he or she could do a better job with this life opportunity than what actually occurred. Sometimes there just doesn't seem to be enough love from family and friends in that person's mind. Mostly, family and friends have no idea how to give the volume of love required. The soul keeps looking for it in all the wrong faces, and hopes are repeatedly dashed. Eventually, the soul gives up and goes home. This situation is not for us to judge. You can do only the best you can and then trust that all is happening in perfect order. That particular soul will receive extensive counseling in the other realms once he or she gets there as the following story illustrates.

There is the interesting story of the man who was so overcome with profound despair about the loss of his business that he committed suicide at his office. He had been taking drugs at the time. As soon as he left his body, he realized that he had not made things better by killing himself, and he was instantly remorseful. As time passed, he went to his house, and he found his wife grieving his death. He also realized that his house had become a profoundly negative place, because of his own drug use. Eventually, he found a medium to help him move on. Just before his transition to the heaven world, he asked this medium to help his wife, for in his violent death, he realized just how much he really did love her and he could see the pain he had caused her. The medium in this case was able to provide him with the guidance on how he could help his wife himself by following the divine guidance he would receive in the heaven world. His wife did receive help and, in fact, left that very negative house the next day. In the experience of his suicide this soul found a way to help himself and his wife to heal.

In the story above, the soul who killed himself learned a tremendous amount about living and dying through this form of death. His family had no idea that he gained so much insight through his own death and may have judged his method of passing quite harshly.

Many relatives of a suicide victim are very angry that this has happened to their family. They are angry at the person who has died. They are angry at their own feelings of inadequacy, and they are really angry that the soul did not ask for help. They may feel humiliated every single time someone asks how their loved one died. Your compassion for friends and family members mourning this unique kind of grief will perhaps help them to accept that sometimes you cannot judge the decisions of another and that perhaps they can heal when they stop judging themselves.

The Karmic Savings and Loan

Understanding karma can put you in a place of deep peace. This peace arises from the profound understanding that every decision you make, every word you say, and every action you do or do not take creates karma in every single moment. This is not something to fear but something to appreciate in its perfection. If you can understand this, then you can apply intelligence to every thought, word, deed, and prayer you think, do, or say. If this intelligence and knowingness is applied honestly and care is always used, then the karma of every moment becomes precious, and the lessons learned from these karmic opportunities become profound. Judgment changes to observation, and observation changes to understanding, and understanding evolves to spiritual growth. Such is the nature of karma. You see that the karma you create in every moment can come back to you with joy or with sorrow and that you control this; no one else does. Karma is always in perfect balance.

Taking this a bit further, one of the beauties in the study of karma is stepping aside, getting yourself out of the way of your perceptions. You never know what karmic issue is being satisfied by a death, by a terrible disease, or by receiving great fortune. Each of us earns the karmic experience we are currently encountering. On a larger scale, understanding that wars, disasters, and wonderful or terrible economic times are also satisfying a karmic balancing requirement. Hence it is in your best interest to step back, ponder, but cease judging the macrocosm of what seems unfathomable at the moment.

Ultimately, it becomes essential to understand three elements of spiritual truth to understand fully the microcosm of death. The first element is reincarnation. The promise of reincarnation is that each soul gets to live again, to try again to learn from the past, and to embrace the future. Families left behind can take some level of comfort in this concept. Even though you may not have this person physically with you, you can embrace the concept that you will possibly get to have another life with him or her again. Hope and faith can spring from this concept.

The second element of understanding death is the concept of karma itself: even this death is happening in perfect balance even though your heart may be breaking.

The final element is the concept of resurrection: we will all get to "live again." Life everlasting is just that—life itself. Death is merely the closing of one door in order to be released from the time beyond physical death and then to opening another door of rebirth, purely for the *opportunity of the next experience.*

This is why it is especially important not to judge a death. Death comes. Not everyone needs 99 experience-filled years. Sometimes you need only a few moments of a specific mortal life to balance a karmic need. Sometimes you need 8 years. In your search for wisdom, you ultimately come to appreciate the mosaic of life and the knowledge that you seldom know all the details of how a situation can be or what it can become. You do not know all the reasons for a life or a death. Observing all that can be is perhaps your wisest choice. Learning detached compassion will be your most precious spiritual practice.

12

PRAYER

Yea, pray oft for those who have passed on. This is part of thy consciousness. It is well. For, God is God of the living. Those who have passed through God's other door are oft listening, listening for the voice of those they have loved in the earth.   **Edgar Cayce Reading 3954-1**

The Science of Prayer

Perhaps it would be good to understand prayer. Prayer is love. When you pray, there is a part of you that opens up to the beauty and tender love of God. When you pray, you invite angels and spiritual beings to come to you. The more you pray the more you become in resonance with these spiritual beings and angels. This divine resonance can assist you in precluding the darkness that comes with a sad event. When you pray, you are hopeful; prayer changes your attitude and lifts you up. The very aspect of prayer opens your heart. The lighter your heart, the less darkness exists there, and the more readily will you and your entire family heal.

When you have experienced a death of any kind, there is a need to open up to the energies of love and light, the energies of God. Understanding all the aspects of prayer will enable you to learn how to help those who are suffering and how to aid them in their desire to relieve this suffering. There is also the aspect of being angry at the situation and perhaps even being angry with

God. The result is that you do not want to pray. You might be wondering why anyone would pray to God since God took your loved one away. This is the very time when you need prayer the most, since you are hurting the most and need to make this divine connection for your deepest healing. This type of healing connects you to the energies of divine love. It is important to remember that God does not punish or hurt you. You are experiencing these levels of pain because you are here to learn from these episodes. Learning and wisdom come from experiencing every facet of life and love.

There is a physics regarding prayer, which revolves around the sending of energy. All thought is energy, so prayer is thought with a positive energy behind it. All prayer is energy. If you spend hours praying, you will find that you feel quite tired. This is because you have used so much physical energy doing what seems to be mental but is, in fact, quite physical. Prayer physically and psychically sends energy to another person or to the universe through the unseen (with ordinary eyes) ether or nether world. What is ether? The ether is an aspect of dimension. You live in the dimension of time and space. However, there is another aspect, and that is one of the angels, of God, or what some belief systems call the afterlife. This is a place with no beginning and no end. It is what you frequently call the other dimensions. This place is also the dimension of ghosts. So when you send energy, it travels through this nether world, this ether, and if you could see prayer energy, it would appear as a beam of white light. When you gather a group of people together to send this energy, quite a powerful white light will be produced in the ether. This is tremendous positive energy: this is prayer!

The Power of Prayer in Healing Grief

How does prayer help to heal grief? Everyone talks about praying for the family of the person, who has died, but what does that mean exactly and how does it really help them? What are you praying for when you pray for the person who has died?

Prayer helps to heal grief by lifting the burdensome weight of the darkness from your aching heart. When you are profoundly sad, you find yourself engulfed in the darkness of your most exquisite pain. When people pray for you, they send you the blessings of their compassionate hearts. It is the brilliant energy of that blessing that begins to dilute the darkness or the hopelessness that you may be feeling.

Prayer sent with love to grieving family members clears the darkness they wake up to each painful day after someone they love has died. Prayer helps them think about what they have to do next. Prayer helps them to be considerate with their children and other family members who may also be grieving. Prayer sent with sincerity enables the family to remember that the often seemingly endless days of the initial moments of death will not, in fact, last forever.

Prayer sent to a person who has died helps that person through the darkness of the initial shadows of death. Prayer sent in love to this person transitioning from life to death to the heaven world helps to light the soul's way.

Prayer sent during any type of grief situation gives people something profoundly important to do when they feel as though they do not know how to help. Prayer sent is so meaningful that, without it, you would find yourself unable to recover with any sense of purpose.

Prayer is the fabric of your healing foundation, and it should begin as soon as you learn of the death.

What Type of Prayer Should You Initially Send?

When you first hear of a death, you are filled with shock. You can't believe that it has happened. Once you are able to take a moment to pray, you may find that the following types of prayer are extremely meaningful.

• You can immediately begin to pray silently to God that light and love be sent to every member of this grieving family.

• You can pray that they have the strength and courage to face the days ahead.

• You can pray that each person remembers how much the deceased loved one adored him or her and the family.

• You can pray that the healing salve of love fills the family's aching, broken hearts.

- You can pray that each person in the family will be clear-headed enough to make the wise decisions that the days ahead will demand, no matter how badly that person feels.
- If you are grieving, you can ask God to help you to make these decisions regarding your deceased loved one.
- If it is you who must bury your son or daughter, husband or wife, parent or friend, pray that you have the wisdom to do the right thing in every moment.
- Pray for the light of knowledge to know what to say to heal your own heart as well as the aching hearts of all those around you.
- You can ask that angels of transition be sent to the soul of the person who has died to light that soul's way to the heaven world so that he or she will not be lost.
- You can even pray to understand the purpose of this death, no matter how senseless or untimely it may seem at the moment.

Prayers that you create from within your heart are the most powerful ones you can send, because they come from your very core, your most compassionate and loving soul. These are the prayers that are sent with the power of love.

What if you are too distraught to create your own prayer? What can you do? There are many wonderful prayer books out there that you can easily use. Whatever effort you make, prayers heal—no matter when, where, or how often you send them.

Where Should You Pray?

There is no special place to pray. Wherever you are, God is there with you, helping you. You can always access this divine guidance. Perhaps the privacy of a bedroom will be best or perhaps outdoors, feeling the power of nature. Some like to be in the deceased person's room, to feel nearer to him or her. There is never any necessity to limit prayers to a physical building, such as a church or temple. Your prayers are heard regardless of the location.

Some people perform private prayer services near bodies of water because water is the symbol of cleansing the soul. Any body of water will do, because the symbol is there. Prayer near an ocean is much better because of the salt air. Salt is additionally cleansing and healing for a grieving person.

Many people like to pray at a cemetery, because they feel nearer to the person at his or her gravesite. Souls do not live in the ground but in the other dimensions, going through all the transitioning actions of the heaven world. If it is possible to pray for the soul in any other place than a cemetery, that is preferable, because that new site helps to eliminate the attachment to the loved one and enables healing to progress for the persons left behind.

Angry Prayer

What if you find yourself furious and enraged with the person who caused the death of your loved one? What if you find yourself thinking bad thoughts about that person? What if the thoughts are really bad— ones that, if they came true by taking physical action, could cause harm or death to the person?

The more you understand the physics of the energy of prayer, the more you can learn to control your thoughts, even your most angry ones. Any violent death is a spiritual challenge at the deepest level. It is at these times when you need prayer more, not less.

The gentlest way to help you overcome the desire to think negative thoughts about another person is to focus positive thoughts on someone else. The urge to judge another is great in these types of situations. That is the spiritual challenge that you must rise up to meet in order to heal yourself, and others.

If you find that it is too difficult to do at first, you must not give up; you must keep pursuing this spiritual challenge to grow past these feelings, even if it takes years. It is only when you can grow past these angry thoughts or angry prayers that you can find your true spiritual self and your own true healing. It can take years to do this. Patience with others and yourself will be required to reach this level of growth and spiritual peace.

Eventually, with time, you may even get to the level of being able to forgive the person who caused the death of your loved one and who has caused you so much pain. The more you focus on positive prayer, the closer you will get to that goal of forgiveness. Once you find that through the power of prayer you have learned to forgive the other person, the cause of your pain, you will literally have set yourself free.

Everyone Is Grieving Something

All people who have ever felt true grief know that, as they begin to talk about their particular pain, they encounter other people who are also grieving. People will tell you about what happened to them. Some people will find themselves going back to their initial sense of grief as they try to comfort you.

The more you work through your grief and talk to others, the more you get a larger sense of the tremendous amount of silent, private grief that literally millions of people are experiencing in every moment. For some, this is a comforting thought. For others, it is no comfort at all.

We are all going to experience some type of grief in our lives. Some experiences just come to a tragic and sudden end. Even though death brings an end to a physical relationship, it does not destroy the love we have for that person. As you experience this, you begin to understand this tremendous dynamic—everyone is grieving something. Perhaps realizing this will enable you to open your compassionate heart to people everywhere who are suffering any type of grief.

Being sensitive to those who are grieving does not mean that you go around feeling sad all the time. It means that you learn to develop a loving heart that readily sends out love and immediately knows to send a prayer whenever you hear of anyone grieving. Eventually this love lives within you, and you begin to send out love to every grieving person as part of your daily prayers. The energy of a compassionate heart helps you to heal as well as to progress spiritually. However, there is even more you can do with the power of your healing prayers.

Impersonal Prayers—Detached Compassion

You can influence the healing of the world by sending it your love, light, and energy. This is the concept of impersonal love or loving kindness in the broadest sense. This type of love creates within you an understanding that everyone suffers and that prayer sent to everyone can help you to develop a sense of detached compassion. In impersonal prayer, you ask nothing for yourself. You realize that, in doing this powerful act, you are sending healing love to murderers, robbers, torturers, people who have wronged you, people who speak ill of you, and people whom you may have hated. You are sending this loving light to all prisoners. You are also sending loving energy regardless of another person's religion or belief (including atheists).

There is the amazing story of a young man who had been tortured as a child by his mother. His father did not help him, and he grew up sad and hurt. Through a chain of events, he learned how to send healing to the world on a continual basis. At first, his hatred of women was so strong that he could not send them healing. It was simply too painful. However, because he was diligent and continued this practice, he began to study the true essence of love, and he realized that he had learned many lessons from this cruel parent. Eventually, he learned to send healing to the entire world, including women. At this point, he grew tremendously in his enlightenment. His heart expanded, and he realized that he had learned how to love on many levels. He was able to forgive this parent, and he no longer hated all women. Such is the power of prayer.

God loves all people impersonally. God does not pick and choose. God loves us all. As an example, many people worry that if their loved one is not of their particular faith, they will not "get into heaven." God would never be concerned whether or not a person chose a particular faith. The light and love of God are impersonal and personal, all at the same time. When you send impersonal love to *all*, you are emulating the power of God's love for all humankind. You are emulating the love Buddha, Jesus, Sri Krishna, and all the Ascended Masters have for all of us all the time. Spiritual beings do not pick and choose whom they will love, and they love us even when we do not pray.

Prayer is the energy vehicle for sending love and light to the world. Developing this spiritual routine will enable you to be far more tolerant and far less judgmental. You will come to realize that the God who lives within you loves everyone. Pray with passion, for passion carries with it energy. It is this energy that specifically spreads your messages of lov-

ing kindness for all, which is a critical and essential part of living only a
life of love.

When Prayers Seem to Go Unanswered

How many times have you heard people comment that they prayed
for something and nothing happened? A loved one is in the hospital in
a life-or-death situation. Only a miracle will do. These people may or
may not have a personal relationship with God, but they have heard
that praying is what you do in this type of situation. Someone is in dire
financial straits, and this person prays for money, a job, or—again—for a
miracle. Frequently, people bargain with God for the expected result.
After praying, they feel that nothing happened. They are bewildered,
confused, and filled with painful conflicting emotions.

All prayers are eventually answered because it is the nature of God
to answer your prayers. However, answers to specific prayers may not
always return to you in the manner or in the time frame you requested,
as the following example illustrates.

One little ten-year-old girl constantly prayed that her father would
be successful, that he would have fame and a retirement. She prayed
that ultimately he would find happiness because he seemed like such
an unhappy dad. She had long suspected that his unhappiness and
insecurity stemmed from the unresolved grief of the death of his own
father when he (her dad) was six-years-old. Eventually, the little girl
grew up, ceased her prayers for her dad, and moved on with her life. As
she began her studies on her spiritual path, she realized that her prayers
for her father were indeed answered. Her father, in divorcing her mother,
finally became financially successful. He became a respected university
professor with tenure and a very secure retirement. He also became
well-known and respected in his field. He achieved a measure of happiness all over a period of some forty years. All the elements of her prayer
were eventually answered with one exception. Her father was never a
happy dad, perhaps because ultimately only he could make that happen and he never quite figured out how to do that or he never finished
working through that old grief that he carried all his life.

Frequently, prayers that ask for a miracle for a dying person are in contradiction to the wants and needs of the dying person. You may be praying for this person's life while he or she is hoping to return to God. How will your prayer be answered in this situation? You would do well to ask yourself if you are praying for the person in front of you or for yourself. Why can't you just let go? If the prayer is for yourself and not in the best interest of the person, you will see that you may gain unexpected insight and understanding. You may feel the ability to actually let go of the dying person so that he or she may cross over in peace. Your prayers were answered, although not in the form you had expected. No prayer goes unanswered.

The fundamental aspect here is to consider carefully the exact focus of your prayer, if it is for a specific person or situation. A prayer is a request to God said with feeling. Creating this prayer can be critical in your ability to see or understand fully the outcome.

When you pray, be clear in your intention: What do you want to happen from this prayer? What situation are you seeking to heal and what outcome do you want? This is an opportunity for sincere faith, an absolute belief in the outcome. The power of your faith is critical to the outcome of the prayer.

Gratitude sent to God for the answer to this prayer will help enhance the power of your request, and you can do this, even as you are praying. However, it is always wise to remember that you cannot request through prayer the abrogation of free will or to force a change in a situation. You can ask through prayer that another person may perhaps have greater insight, or that peace may come to them or that pain and difficulty may not be so severe. You can also pray that wonderful things happen to another person.

The other aspect is one of being grateful. Even if you are grieving, there will be something you can find for which you may be grateful, even if you are in tremendous pain. Perhaps someone else was saved even if your loved one was not. Perhaps complete strangers came to your aid when you least expected it. Emergency personnel may have really done a superb job helping your loved one, and yet he or she still died. You still need to be grateful to all who helped you, and in that attitude of gratitude, you will find light and healing. Prayers of gratitude themselves can take you to that healing place.

Believing Your Prayers

Do you believe what you pray? Really believe? Believe with an unshakable faith? Does praying make you think or act differently? Many people attend church regularly every Sunday and often attend several times during the week, and yet, once they leave the confines of the religious building, they return to their old habits of perhaps questionable business practices, bigotry, gossip, and separatism. Many never see the power of prayer as lifting them up, encouraging them to *act differently* toward family and friends, perhaps more tolerant, patient, and, above all, wise.

The purpose of prayer is to uplift everyone, to transcend the physical world, and to take you to the higher planes, while you still reside in a physical body. Prayer offers hope, promise, protection, love, guidance, healing, and a deeper understanding as well as faith in the concept of life everlasting. With prayer, you connect and talk to God. Yet, even as you do this, perhaps you are also afraid. What if this is a fear of death and of actually enjoying life everlasting? Gently release this fear. Everyone will experience death and when you can accept that inevitability with a sense of grace, you will find a greater sense of peace.

What if there was no prayer? You cannot imagine being unable to talk to God. Prayer creates a form and a forum for speaking to God. You do not need a massive structure that makes you feel small to speak to God. You do not need anyone's permission to speak to God. You do not need an intermediary to speak to God.

- Pray in a field of flowers. Feel the color and fragrance of a miracle.
- Pray in bed at night and know the security of never being alone, for God is with you.
- Pray with a child and help him or her connect to God.
- Pray with a friend and help this person reconnect with the voice of love.
- Pray with a parent and remind him or her of your love and of God's love.
- Pray in a forest and hear God's voice in the gentle breeze.
- Pray for the world that there will be peace and joy.
- Pray every single day of the year and you will know the pleasure

and power of spiritual practice.

- Pray with purpose and take on the suffering of the world.
- Pray for your most powerful enemy and pray that this person may know love.
- Pray with gratitude for all that you know, all that you are, and all that is before you on every realm.
- Pray to your angels with thanks for their vigilance for you.
- Pray for all those who have died. Pray that they have found peace and enlightenment.
- Pray for guidance from God so that you may know and understand love.
- And when you have prayed and prayed, you will begin to understand the meaning of living and teaching only love. This prayer is for those who believe that you are here only for service.

Edgar Cayce's Prayer for the Dead

Father, in Thy love, Thy mercy, be Thou near those who are in—and have recently entered—the borderland. May I add, when Thou seest that Thou canst use me.   281-15

13

SERVICE

If ye would have peace, *make* peace in the lives of others.
If ye would have harmony, *make* harmony or harmonious
experiences in the lives of others.

Edgar Cayce Reading 1073-3

There are many forms of service, and there are many ways that someone can perform service. Perhaps the following examples may offer some insight to some of the simplest yet most meaningful ways, in those ordinary day–to–day moments, where one person really helps another. All of the stories below are true; however, the names have been changed to protect individual privacy.

The tall lieutenant knocked on the Commander's door and asked if he could speak with her for a moment. She had been expecting him. As he sat down, she looked at his body language: he walked heavily for having such a slight frame. He seemed to have a shadow of fear with him, wearing it like a cloak around his slender shoulders.

"How can I help you, Lieutenant?" She asked.

"I need to know if you will accept me as a transfer from my submarine to your training command for limited duty. We just discovered that my daughter Bonnie has leukemia. Monday was her first birthday. What a tough thing to learn on what should have been a happy day! The doctors say that I will really need to be with my wife and daughter as they will begin chemotherapy on

Bonnie immediately to stop this aggressive cancer. Is there a place for me here? The XO (Executive Officer) on my submarine says it's going to suck when she dies. Commander, do you think my daughter is going to die? Can you help me?"

She did not hesitate, "Of course, you can be transferred here; of course, we will accept you as part of our command. I will place you in the training section. I have a good-sized staff there, and we will be able to cover you when you need to be away for your daughter. Lt. Doss, I do not know what the future holds for your little girl, but we, this command, will stand with you as you go through this. Keep me informed daily if necessary of what is happening."

Lt. Doss looked at her with sensitive brown eyes as he thanked her. Then he left. Over the coming days, he kept his word, always keeping his new Executive Officer (XO) informed of what was happening with his precious daughter. Many times after negative reports would come in about his daughter's therapy, the LT would visit his XO. Sometimes the tears would come, and she would just let him have those private moments of grieving. He wanted to be strong for his wife and daughter, but he needed those moments where he could let down his "tough guy, I can handle it" image and just be a sad dad.

As the weeks turned to months and all the chemotherapy and the bone marrow transplants failed, the LT began to talk to the Commander, his XO daily. Sometimes, he would call her from the hospital at night telling her about how hard it was to watch in despair, as his daughter's life began to leave her. Finally the moment came when he and his beloved wife said enough: there really is nothing more that can be done. Bonnie is dying. The LT told his XO that they could not bear to watch another procedure, another injection, or violation to Bonnie's little body. They knew they were ready to let her go. Bonnie knew it, too. On the evening of her second birthday, she was in her Dad's arms and turned to all the nurses and thanked them. She told her parents she loved them, and then she simply slipped away.

As the LT called the Commander and explained his daughter's last moments, she could hear that in the sadness of the moment, there was a release of the stress from the last year. She listened over the next weeks as he shared his grief with her. He and his wife were so glad their daughter was out of pain, but they missed her terribly. They missed the life they were never going to have with her. He also began to be concerned about his career. He literally had lost a year of his military life. How could he ever regain this? His Commander assured him that, while this was not necessarily a year of career enhancing military action, he would not be punished for guiding his family through this life crisis.

What he did not know was the degree to which his boss, his XO had run interference to ensure that his career was, in fact, not derailed. Much behind the scenes work was done to keep his career on track. He was an exceptionally fine officer who was having a horrendous year, but that did not mean that his career would be allowed to die with his daughter. He needed an advocate and his Executive Officer, his Commander, was that advocate for an entire year. This is where the real service of his Commander came in: she made sure that at the end of this, he would still have a career, that the insight and wisdom that the LT had gained from this experience would not be lost to the Navy. . . and it wasn't. Lt. Doss went on to have an Executive Officer and then a Commanding Officer tour on a submarine. He and his wife went on to have more children. They moved forward with their lives, and they continued to apply the lessons learned from this experience to their military life. Lt. Doss continued to serve his country on many insightful levels. Often the service one person performs for another may appear transparent, simple in fact, but the ramifications of that service will truly echo out for a lifetime.

The next example of service is the story of what one neighbor can do for another.

When her doorbell rang late one chilly January afternoon, Marie opened the door to find her dearest neighbor Joan literally sobbing on her front steps. Joan was sobbing so hard that she could not stand or speak. It took some minutes of chest heaving and hard crying to be able to even get Joan moved into the house.

After almost twenty more minutes of this, Marie was convinced that one of Joan's sons had died or that her husband had died. Surely, someone must have died for her neighbor's sobs to be this severe. But no one had died. Her pets were all safe and alive. Finally, after doctoring her friend with Rescue Remedy and hugs, the story finally emerged.

It was Joan's twenty-year marriage that had died that day. Apparently, Joan's husband had been having an affair. On that day he had finally decided to end it with his wife and family and called Joan from the airport to tell her. He was a salesman, and he was flying to another city. He told his wife he wouldn't be coming home and that he didn't love her anymore. Then he hung up. Joan had no idea this was coming.

Joan went into shock as the cascade of ramifications swept her like some ugly black wave, hitting her again and again, until she was literally drowning in darkness. Marie could feel the volume of despair filling her friend as she watched all the light leave those beautiful eyes. The friend she knew and loved died that day and a very different woman took her place.

Marie did not ask her friend how she could help her, she simply helped her. In a divorce situation, there is no particular end. In divorce, all the players are continually present making healing a very different challenge than death. Marie's job was to help her friend return to balance, by working to understand why this happened, what she could learn from it, and how to find light and happiness in her life again. Marie's job was to faithfully remind her friend that happiness was a probability, not an impossible dream.

In divorce, often what starts out as a really bad event becomes increasing terrible over time as the full scope of the emotional betrayal becomes apparent. And that is what happened in this case. Marie's friend needed her love and support for many, many years, but not the kind of support that demonized the former husband. Joan needed the kind of support that empowered her to understand why her husband did this. This was the support that Marie provided, month after month, year after year.

When people are married to each other, they have one personality, but when they separate and then divorce from each other, it is almost as if they forget who they were as they often become someone else completely. Marie understood that this was Joan's experience. Marie's job was to be a friend, to be there for Joan, and to encourage her to believe in the possibility of healing her shattered heart, even as she was grieving. Joan did begin to believe this, and she did heal. The process took many years, because human beings cannot just "get over" love betrayed. They have to grieve it, learn from it, and then agree within themselves to forgive the other person and to heal it. That process takes as long as it takes, and in this case, Marie's friendship with Joan turned out to be a tremendous service.

This final example is another military story, but it is the story of any group of people helping a family in need. It is also an example of how an employer and co-workers can really help an employee in need.

Petty Officer Jones and her husband woke up to the acrid smell of smoke. They grabbed their pets and raced past growing flames, narrowly escaping their fire-engulfed building.

They lost everything including all their wedding presents with some still unwrapped from the ceremony only a few weeks ago. They lost every stick of furniture, every wedding photo, and every pot and pan. They didn't have that much to begin with, but they had worked very hard for the little they did have.

They also realized, to their utter dismay, that they both lost all of their uniforms. How would they report for duty? Immediately, both of them called their respective commands and informed them of what had happened and the extent of their losses.

They were understandably a bit overwhelmed with the shock and the grief of their situation.

The military service is often about service to each other, as much as it is service to this country. In this case, Petty Officer Sara Jones and her husband, Petty Officer Howard Jones, each worked for a different command at the Charleston, South Carolina Naval Base. Both Commanding Officers assigned a person within their respective commands to coordinate assistance for this couple.

As bad as the couple felt about their losses, they soon discovered that their "military family" was really there for them. Military and civilian members from both organizations donated food, clothing, uniforms, kitchen supplies, and furniture. The Navy put them in the Navy Lodge until the couple could find suitable housing. Money was collected to enable them to purchase new things. The Navy Relief Society and the Red Cross both gave them assistance.

The couple learned a great deal from this experience. Even though they lost material "things," they were utterly astounded to see how very generous their friends and coworkers were. People they did not know gave them money and sent encouraging cards. Petty Officers Sara and Howard Jones discovered just how blessed they were to have such tremendous support. The fire as it turned out was not a good event and it was not a bad event. Eventually they came to look at it as an amazing experience in how an event such as a fire, can bring out the best in people.

They also learned when the head of any organization, military or not, steps up to the plate and shows leadership in helping his own people, that the entire organization benefits. Morale was really high as everyone pitched in to lend a hand and help this couple. It made people feel good about themselves, and it made them proud of their organization. Such can be the subtle but important byproducts of service.

What Is Service?

Sometimes, service just happens. Doing service doesn't start out as a conscious thought, and at times, you find yourself doing service when you least expect it. This is what makes helping people special and rewarding, whether you are the giver or the receiver. When you believe you are incapable of carrying out a particular service and then find that you are completing the task, the resulting feeling is even more special. Oftentimes, the most difficult and yet rewarding type of service is that given to those who are grieving.

- A friend calls when you have had a bad day of fighting back tears from oncoming grief waves. She listens with sympathy, doing what she can and sending you her love.
- You visit a friend in the hospital who is dying. You may think you do not know what to say, but then suddenly the words of comfort just come.
- A neighbor's cherished dog dies. You go over, hold her hand, and let her cry. You remind her not to be embarrassed that she loved her faithful dog this much.

All of those examples above are caring actions and natural responses. You live with people; you help them. Why is it even necessary to define such natural responses? It is important to do this, because these responses cause you to recognize and to appreciate their tremendously positive impact. It is possible to heal the world, one person at a time, with even the tiniest gesture of love and care.

Service is the act of giving of yourself, without expectation of reward or even of acknowledgment, for the betterment of your fellow human beings. It is offering your kindness in the smallest ways so that another person may be helped. It is an act of selflessness. However, service surpasses even the boundaries of these definitions.

The wonderful fact is that most people do service daily and don't think twice about it. A good majority of the population of the world is made up of people willing to do service for others. If the world were not filled with these people, you would live on a planet dominated by chaos and greedy selfishness, without any semblance of courtesy or small acts of kindness. But can you provide more service to the world? Yes, and the more you do, the better the world becomes.

Each small act of kindness is dynamic in its potential. The more we help, the more we want to help. The more we look for the goodness in the person in front of us, the more goodness we can find. Even in those challenging moments, when words fail us, our generous heart and our courageous desire to do service carry us to the next level of our own goodness and eases even the most difficult times.

Service to those who are dying and to families who are grieving becomes a unique form of support. The gentle kindness of a friend, neighbor, or family member becomes precious in the ordinariness of the action. In grieving, there is the opportunity to accept and to perform service.

Why Does Real Service Feel Terrific?

Real service is terrific because it exemplifies the very best part of us—the part that we can be proud of and humble about all at the same time.

In the movie called *Groundhog Day*, Bill Murray plays a despicable television reporter who, all day long, takes glee in alienating everyone he meets. He is intensely disliked. During an assignment to cover a story about Punxsutawney Phil, the ground hog, he relives the day over and over. Time stands still; the tape just keeps repeating again and again. He finally figures out that he has to change his attitude about others before he can get beyond this particular day. He starts doing service, a tiny bit at first, and discovers to his horror that he likes it. The more service he does, the more people start to like him. Then life around him changes all in that one cold and frosty day. Finally, he figures out that life is only about service, the pleasure it brings others, and the difference it makes. He discovers the genuine happiness he feels by helping others, and finally he is able to move on to a new day.

You are here to serve others with a positive heart. Once service becomes part of your makeup, your very being, then you can discover a true happiness you never thought possible. You start out by helping people, because it is the right thing to do. Then you do it because it feels good, and finally you do it without thinking about it because it is inherently a part of your nature, it lives within you.

There is a remarkable side effect to doing service. It begins to heal you. As you help someone else who is grieving, you find that you begin to feel your own long-buried sadness coming to the surface. As you hug another, a part of you is nurtured. In giving love, you are also receiving love and healing a part of yourself that may still be in pain. Many parents, who have experienced the death of a child, find themselves reaching out to other families who go through that same experience. These generous parents understand that pain, and they remember what helped them, so they reach out to other families. That shared experience becomes knowledge, wisdom of what to do, and how to help an-

other family in their darkest of moments. Helping someone else understand that exquisite loss means that you have to face your own grief all
over again. Your willingness to help with an open heart is an essential
measure of your own healing progress.

How powerful is this? Consider that one family which had just suffered the sudden death of their son, met with a family who six years
previously had experienced the death of their very young daughter.
The family still in shock looked at the kindness and compassion that
the visiting family was offering and realized that there was hope that
they too could find that healing path. Such is the opportunity for each
family gently embracing the power of shared experience.

Service heals parts of your soul you didn't know needed healing and
in ways you couldn't imagine. Sometimes simply reading about positive acts of loving service shows you the benefits of that service. You
may find yourself emulating these positive acts when similar situations
arise. Someone else lit the path, and you continue to carry the light
forward.

Service opens all the parts of your heart and allows you to feel what
other people are feeling, in a sympathetic way. You can never fully know
what that other person is feeling, but you can open yourself up to understanding the need for help. When your heart grows inside you and
you know the joy of helping others, especially when it is a challenging
grief situation, you grow to new spiritual levels. The most profoundly
beneficial level of assistance any individual can provide is service to
those who are grieving and to those who have died.

Service in the Grieving Process

When you are called upon to assist someone in a situation involving
death, you may want to take a quiet moment and honestly ask yourself
how you feel about what you are going to be asked to do. Are you
going to be comfortable walking through the front door of a house
where a child has died? Are you able to handle the tears grown men
will be shedding? Are you going to be able to cry and not feel embarrassed by the well-spring of emotion that may come from within you?
Do you have that much courage?

If you have to break the news to a child or teenager that a sibling or parent has died, you have to rehearse what you are going to say, how you are going to say it, and how you are going to handle that child's response. You are going to have to consider that your actions in this moment will be extremely powerful for that child and will be remembered by this little one or teenager for a very long time. The wisdom with which you choose your words will be critically important. Now is the time to pray for the wisdom to choose the best words to get you though this tender, yet powerful moment.

Helping someone grieve may cause you to question your own beliefs in God, in the afterlife. Discussions may come up regarding this topic. Are you going to be comfortable with this line of thought? Can you listen to people's anger and not judge them?

When you are speaking to a person in mourning, are you at ease with asking God or your angels for just the right words to say to them? Are you comfortable with your own level of spirituality?

Are you able to provide comfort to a friend whose spouse committed suicide? Ask yourself, can you do it? Can you look at his or her tear-stained face and reach out with all of your heart? Are you going to be able to find it within yourself to help guide your friend away from judging the traumatic event and to find compassion for the person who took his or her own life?

If your teenager has a friend who committed suicide, are you going to sit your son down and be open to discussing this crisis with him? Even if you do not know this other teenager, your son does and is profoundly affected by it. Your courage in addressing this matter with your son will win his respect and will enable both of you to grow.

If your daughter comes to you crying that her best friend has died in a car accident, how are you going to comfort her? What words are you going to say to help your beloved daughter to heal? Are you planning on being patient with her while she goes through the grieving process? Will you join her in searching for answers? Will you give her the best of yourself?

Grief, death, trauma are never convenient. Life changing events happen to you while you are making other plans. Yet, these moments are the opportunities for your greatest service to your friends and family.

These are the occasions for your greatest growth and soul evolution.

Service in Relationships

Marriage is a roller coaster of emotional ups and downs. In many scenarios each spouse may depend on the other to be up or to help "cheer up" the other in difficult situations. Good marriages do this. However, when death touches your marriage or your relationship, you are both going to be down, but even then, it depends on the type of death.

If your wife's parent dies, she will be more grief-stricken than you probably are, and your ability to help her may define your finest service to her. Your patience with her during this time will be invaluable. She will long remember how you helped her, even though you may have felt clumsy about it at the time. Your heart was there for her. You held her when she cried at night. You brought her tissues and tea when she just had to sit and talk about how much she misses her mom or dad. You managed the kids so that she could help her surviving parent cope with the death. You were fantastic. That is service in a relationship.

Suppose your best friend dies. He was your best sports buddy. Perhaps you had been friends for decades. His death hits you hard. You don't really show your grief and shrug off your emotional pain. You are the classic "tough guy." Your wife's service to you will be to understand that you cannot talk about the death of your friend until you are ready. She can feel your moods, and she respects your needs. This is huge service to you. If she pestered you to "talk about it, to get it out, and to cry," you would close yourself up tighter in that clam shell and never open up. She leaves the door open to talk, but she doesn't drag you through it. The beauty of your relationship is that, in this case, her love is respectful of your processing time.

Men process grief differently from women. Men often take awhile to decide how they feel about a deep sadness. Frequently, all women want to do is talk about what has happened. In the case of the death of a child, this will be a difficult situation. No matter what the method of death for your child, there may be times of awkwardness as each of you walks your healing path. Perhaps the best service in this type of scenario is to be mindful never to blame the other spouse for what has happened. Even if it seems to be your spouse's fault that the child died, your spouse will already be blaming himself or herself profoundly. Your service, and this is the hardest service, will be to reserve judgment of your husband or wife for whatever happened. Nothing will return that child to you. The goodness that you had before the death will be required to carry you to the other side of the most profound pain you will have ever known. Perhaps the most precious and hard-won lesson of any child's death is to go on living after the one you loved so exquisitely is gone. This is the time for your greatest compassion, and it may be the most challenging time you will ever know.

Whatever your relationship with another person, child/parent, parent/grandparent, brother/sister, whatever it is, let patience, kindness, and consideration be the building blocks that you use to chart the new course of your relationships. You still need each other, and that need will help you both to heal if you use wisdom to light your way.

Receiving Service in the Form of Grief Counseling

It has never been a particularly nice feeling to need help, especially when you are grieving. It is stigmatized in society. People who need help seem powerless, vulnerable, and unable to handle their own lives. However, when you find yourself in a position where you are grieving, you are seldom prepared and oftentimes do not know how to deal with the mountain of emotions that continue to sweep you. Mostly, you just tell people that you are doing okay and that you do not need any help, but inside you feel like you are dying.

However, if you are wise, you will ask yourself if perhaps you could possibly benefit from grief counseling. Needing grief counseling does not mean that you "cannot handle your grief." Receiving grief counseling means that you realize you just need to get a different point of view on your level of suffering. Because you are so mired in your suffering, you just can't quite get yourself out of the way.

Perhaps someone else can offer a different perspective, based on years of hearing the despondency of other people. Good grief counselors know that sometimes the person in deep mourning has to find someone, who is not emotionally drowning with them, to help them with that life ring. In other words, if you are in a life raft of grieving people, it may be hard to get another person who is literally "in the same boat" to be able to offer you any meaningful perspective on your healing path. You often need a break from the grief of friends, family members, and even co-workers. You need someone to help you understand your thoughts, fears, and possibly guilt feelings.

Grief counseling will enable you to feel lighter, get a lot of clogging emotion off your chest, and very possibly avoid clinical depression. This perspective will enable you to help your friends, family, and co-workers on their healing path because of your leadership in this area. You are publicly stating that it is okay to get help. Your actions will give other people the courage to ask for help in the future should they encounter a similar situation.

Understanding Suffering

All suffering has meaning. If it did not, then you simply would not have that experience. However, when you are in the midst of suffering, it is very hard to see any value in death, divorce, illness, disease, financial setbacks, accidents, natural disasters, or wars. All you see and feel is pain. Frequently in the midst of your most profound pain, you are called upon to perform service for someone else. You may be extremely tired, sick, penniless, and depressed, and yet you are called. God offers opportunities for service when you least expect them. It is during these opportunities that you frequently find the most meaning in adversity.

For example, let us say that your Dad died suddenly, and that you are very involved with settling his estate. It has been about four months since his death and you are working hard to process your grief, when your brother calls to say that he has broken his arm and asks you to come and help him. Of course you go, even though you are still reeling from your father's death. Within three months of this event, your other brother becomes very ill, and you are asked to help with his care, too. In each case, you rise to the occasion. This is service, and this is the nature of loving another even when you don't think you can handle anything else.

Every facet of suffering offers you an opportunity not only to understand yourself but also to appreciate those around you. The suffering anyone feels with profound grief teaches you an amazing amount of information about love and loss. Even though you may know this fact abstractly, when you experience it firsthand, either by helping someone or by receiving the help yourself, you are in a tremendous learning environment. For example, perhaps you did not have a good relationship with your own mother, but when your friend's mother dies, she is devastated. Her relationship with her mother was tremendous. From your friend's grief, you learn what a good relationship looks like and how much that mother/daughter connection meant to them. The actions of helping your friend are very enlightening for you.

You heal suffering when you look for the lessons to be learned from the experience—no matter how painful. It is this learning that opens your compassionate heart and allows you to acquire wisdom. What wisdom might you find from this type of experience? Perhaps you learned how many other people have had loved ones die. Perhaps someone you always thought of as hardhearted, may have been among the saddest and most compassionate at your situation. They really did have a soft spot in their heart. People, whom you thought would have been really helpful, were intimidated by your experience and simply slipped out of your life. You learned how much your loved one meant to other people. Perhaps you had no idea how truly wonderful they were. As you observe these things without judgment, you may find that you are growing from the experience.

When Service Is Really Hard

It is in those instances, when service is the hardest, that it is also the time of greatest spiritual potential. When your heart is breaking and the enormity of the event takes your breath away, this is the time of your most profound opportunity. Standing up to the moment is often the very reason for the moment. This moment is when life takes on deeper meaning; this moment is when your heart expands and you can grow. Your service will also provide an important example to others so that they can know that service action is possible, even at the most difficult moments.

How does it look if you have a friend with AIDS? If you help him through the dying process, will people judge you? Or how does it look when you visit a co-worker or friend who has had an abortion? How can you help her? What can you say to her and what will people say about you? How do you help the person to heal who accidentally left his or her child unattended in a swimming pool, and the child died? What do you say to that person?

Perhaps another view is this—what kind of test or experience is this for each of us? If you can get to the point where only the person in front of you matters, and not what people think, then you have learned one of the lessons of this difficult experience. This is also a time to pray with all of your heart for the right words to say and the most beneficial actions to take in each moment.

The Miracle of Service

Though you may feel that you are performing a small service, it may seem like a miracle to the person receiving that service. When you perform service out of pure love, it is definitely a miracle. "Miracles occur naturally as expressions of love. The real miracle is the love that inspires them. In this sense everything that comes from love is a miracle."[10]

You wonder just what to do in any given—perhaps awkward—situation. You question what comes next. You often ask why it is you who has been selected to be of service.

All miracles mean life, and God is the Giver of life. His Voice will direct you very specifically. You will be told all you need to know . . . Miracles are healing because they supply a lack; they are performed by those who temporarily have more for those who temporarily have less.[11]

This is important to understand because many times you may have no idea how to handle a problem. Ask God for help, and it will be forthcoming. As you help, so will you also receive it.

Therefore, service is an aspect of giving of yourself. If you cannot physically be with someone, prayer is most important because it can be a service performed at a distance. Thought transformed into prayer is a miracle. The energy of prayer travels through time and space at the speed of thought. You can perform prayer anytime and anywhere. The more fervent the prayer is, the more powerful the miracle.

> A miracle is a service. It is the maximal service you can render to another. It is a way of loving your neighbor as yourself. You recognize your own and your neighbor's worth simultaneously . . . Miracles are examples of right thinking, aligning your perceptions with truth as God created it.[12]

When Service Becomes Part of You

- When service becomes part of who you are, you are able to look closely at others and see many of the finer points of living.
- Service is seeing life as it really is with no illusions.
- Service is learning to be honest with yourself.
- Service is learning your limitations with grace.
- Service is joy in the good fortune of another.
- Service is gratitude for small things.
- Service is truth and honesty.
- Service is accepting what you cannot change.
- Service is honoring the small things, the day-to-day.
- Service is accepting death and letting go.
- Service is learning about the Creator and the beauty of all things.
- Service is asking questions and seeking answers for yourself and others.
- Service is a life lesson. Take the leap of faith, trust in the divine, and see how wonderful you truly are.

And when service has become part of your very being, you will know the meaning of living through loving service.

14

MOVING FORWARD

The passing in, the passing out, is as but the summer, the fall, the spring; the birth into the interim, the birth into the material. **Edgar Cayce Reading 281-16**

What Moving Forward Means

When disaster, death, or loss comes to you, and you are brought to an abrupt halt, there is a feeling of chaos in your life. Where once you planned weeks, months, possibly years in advance, now you find it excruciating to move from minute to minute. What will it take to restart the normally functioning engines of your life? Where is the key for that starter?

You are the key to the starter. Look in the mirror and see your goodness, your kindness, and your courage. Remember that you are still that same person of wonderful qualities, you are just profoundly sad right now, bewildered really at all that has happened to you and around you. Remind yourself that tomorrow will be a little tiny bit better than today. Next week, things will be better still. You will have made it through the funeral; you will have sent the helpful relatives home, and you will look around you to decide what to do next.

If you experienced a natural or financial disaster, wherever you are, you have to do the same things. You have to decide your priorities of where you will live, how you will manage your finances, and what can you salvage from this personal disaster. You will also be sorting out who is helping you and what your personal and emotional resources are or will be.

If you are going through the early days of becoming divorced, remember that you are still a loveable person and that a year from now or five years from now, you will gaze back at this day and marvel at your courage. Anticipate that moment of your healing.

Anticipating Healing, Anticipating Hope

Hope is life's longing for expression. Hope is the crocus bulb, full of gorgeous potential, hidden under the snows of winter. Hope has to survive the cold, possibly freezing ground, and wait patiently for the Earth to warm enough for it to dare to poke through soil. It takes time to work through the dark rich soil, sometimes a cold snap freezes it back to the ground, but eventually, with enough warm, sunny days, the bulb pours its energy into life itself and bursts forth in bloom.

Perhaps you are like that plucky little bulb. You may feel buried by the enormity of your life-changing event, chilled by the reality that your life will never be the same, yet hope stubbornly lives within you. Your goodness cannot stay buried forever. The glorious personality that has always defined you has to come out. Someone smiles at you, and you realize that you are smiling back at him. You become the sunlight for your own awakening.

Slowly, delicately, you can feel some part of yourself returning, and you recognize it. It is you and yet different. You have come to accept that you are not ever going to be the same. You are wiser now, still sad, but perhaps you look at things with a more sage approach, but not a bitter one. Bitterness robs healing and the hope for energetic potential. Bitterness feeds your darkness. Hope gently lightens your heart. Hope anticipates that there will come a day when healing will be felt, and, even though it isn't quite today, perhaps it will be tomorrow.

Loving More Heals Your Heart

Here is an interesting experiment to try. Close your hand. Make a fist. Note how much light is in your hand. None. No light can ever get into that hand. Now keep your hand closed. See how long you can do this. Eventually, keeping your hand closed becomes profoundly painful because it is an artificial action. In the same way, being closed to the light is not a natural place to be.

Now open your hand as wide as possible. How much light is in your hand now? There is as much light as you can possibly imagine in your hand. Now keep your hand open in a natural position. See how long you can do this. Eventually, you realize that you can do this literally forever. Being open to the light is a natural place to be.

Light is love inside your heart. The more light you allow into your heart, the more you can heal and the more comfortable you can become over time. Opening up to all the love from friends, family, co-workers, and even courteous strangers is a very natural place to be when you feel normal. But being in a place of grief is not a "normal" place to be. You have to decide that you are returning to that normal loving place and that this is where you are going to live for the rest of your life.

The light you invite with this courageous decision will show people that healing from grief is possible. Your grief experience will have made you a stronger, more grateful person. You know intimately how precious love is, and you continue to love with ever increasing passion. You appreciate how valuable life is, and you are living it all the way. Love is the way. Love is the answer. On your days of powerful grief waves, cry, dry your tears and fill yourself with the most powerful love you can, and then project this love to the whole world.

Maybe the first time, you can't do this, or maybe even the second time, but eventually, the love you project will heal you because you will become light itself. Perhaps you may think that this is impossible to do, but at the end of this book, there is a jewel, a quiet profile in the courage of one amazing man who is doing just that: he has become the soul of love and compassion, caring and kindness. Perhaps his example may light your way.

Create a Light Work Template

You create your realities. You just never imagined that the reality of this physical and/or emotional tidal wave would ever be one you would have to live with, but it is. So, the challenge of healing is to create a Light Work Template for yourself and your family if they would like to participate. This template is a slate of actions, which specifically create a healing framework and a path into this strange new future.

• Decide that each new day will be a better day than the one before it. Say to yourself before you fall asleep that *tomorrow will be a better day*.

• Decide that you are going to smile several times each day, even if you have to force it. Smiles light your heart, and they help everyone around you to relax a little. Smiles also give friends and family members unspoken permission to begin to feel cheerful again.

• Say a prayer morning and evening by yourself, with your children, or with your spouse that goes something like this: *Day-by-day in every way, I am getting better and better and better. Every day I am healing on deeper and deeper levels.* Perhaps you won't mean it or believe it at first, but, as time goes on, you will. This concept of possibility will begin to live within you.

• Decide that you are going to continue to build a wonderful life, even though the person, or house, or job that you love so much is now gone.

• Realize that moving into your future is inevitable and is in no way disloyal to the loved one who is no longer with you. Picking up the pieces of your life and living again, laughing again will not betray the love or the memory of your beloved.

• Recognize that moving forward means that you have placed all the treasured memories of your loved one, or your previous home, in a very safe place in your heart. Moving forward means that you take all those treasured memories with you. You don't leave them behind. The memories of your loved one's personality live in your heart. You can feel them every day. Moving forward with your life just means that you are carrying those precious experiences with that person with you. This is not attachment; it is the reality that your life with that person physically ended but that your love and memories are what you keep forever.

- Consider beginning a simple spiritual routine that sends healing to every other grieving person all over the world. Perhaps you can send him or her love and healing in the name of the one who has died.
- Wherever possible, spend time in nature with family and friends. Take long walks, stand by a stream, and watch as life around you keeps going. The rivers of life do not reverse themselves; they just keep moving forward because that is the way of life.
- Do service for others in small, manageable ways. This really gets you back into that loving place and reminds you just what a good person you are and how much you are needed by those around you.
- You may discover that someone you know also feels the touch of death as someone close to them dies. Your loving heart may want to reach out to them even though you are not sure how you can really help. Reaching out, in and of itself, is a healing action and the other person or family will appreciate it.
- Make a conscious decision to create holidays that will be just wonderful for your whole family, even though this may seem extremely difficult. This is a service of love you give to those loveable ones who are living through this life challenge with you. You have to make a conscious decision to do this, because celebrating after a death seems unnatural, but it is normal to honor the celebrations of life. Ask everyone to work on this with you; lead the way.
- If you can cook, go ahead and make something. The creative act of cooking will feel familiar, and your family will appreciate it. Even if you still don't feel like eating it, your family will sense the courage of your efforts.
- Invite someone to have lunch; take in a ball game; go to the movies with you. Your friend will be surprised by the invitation and will hopefully meet you. Make every effort to enjoy this time with your friend.
- Sing to the tunes your loved one loved. At first, it sounds impossible, but eventually, over time, you will be able to sing, or hum, or hear that favorite song, and you will be able to smile when you hear that tune, in loving, not painful memory. Again, this is another modest measure of how well you are healing. Again, it is leadership for your friends and family.

- Play beautiful music in your home all the time, happy, upbeat themes or classical music. Music lightens the soul and will help transmute the feeling of grief in your home.

Oftentimes, it feels awkward to return to doing the ordinary things you used to do before your life changed. However, as you gently nudge yourself to do each one in time, you will be able to see that you are making important steps in your healing path. Moving forward means you put yourself in first gear and just go slowly for awhile until you finally feel that the engines of your own life can begin to literally gear up to embrace the new life you are going to be living following this now new and often uncharted path.

Living Again

There is an eloquent line from the movie *The Shawshank Redemption*: "Get busy livin' or get busy dyin.'" Getting busy means that living and loving again are the inherent spiritual and emotional answers. Giving to others is the ultimate path to embracing a newly healed life. These actions honor your experience, honor the one who is not here, and allow you the grace with which to move forward with your life.

Now is the time to become the true lightworker, courageously working toward the greatest good, the wisest path, and the most compassionate heart. At the end of the day, at the end of a life, these are the qualities that ultimately heal grief.

PRAYERS
by
Tina Erwin

A Prayer for Understanding

Dearest Lord,
I most humbly pray that
I may understand the loving ways of
perfect order.
I pray that I may understand the
cosmic view.
I pray that I may find meaning in my
pain and hope in my yearning heart
at the transition of my
precious loved one [Name].
Please grant me strength and insight
so that in my healing path,
I may be of service
to others.

A Prayer for [Name of Person]

Dearest Lord above,
I ask that you take my precious
loved one [Name]
into your loving arms.
I ask that angels teach and guide her (him)
in the ways of love and hope.
I ask that she (he) know of my continued love
and joy in having had her (him) in my life.
May the love she (he) gave me be shared with
all the people in the worlds
of Heaven and Earth.

A Quiet Profile in Courage

Every now and then, you come upon those who have suffered the experience of death in their family, and you wonder how they did it. You wonder how they managed to pick themselves up and to move forward with each new day, and yet you know, or you think you know, what they must be suffering.

Sometimes, you may stop and think that you are not sure how you would handle, say, the death of your child, thinking that this type of loss might be all this person has experienced. And yet, many times, you would be wrong.

Sometimes a person has suffered, as in the case of one particular man, the deaths of many family members. This person watched as, one by one, in the normal course of events, all of his grandparents died. Even though this would appear to be the "natural" order of things, it did not diminish the love or the grief that this young man would have suffered at each passing.

What if this person also had experienced the sudden loss of his younger brother? He would have watched as his sister-in-law picked herself up and put her life back together with her two young children. Imagine his grief at watching her, as well as watching his parents grieve for the loss of their son. Imagine his own pain at the loss of his brother. Grief is experienced in many ways when a family member dies. Individuals grieve for their own sense of loss and then grieve for the pain all of their family members are feeling.

Within ten years or so, this particular man's father also died, a very beloved dad. He helped his dad through that final process. He spoke at his funeral with deep affection.

Now imagine what it must be like to have experienced the loss of your precious six-year-old daughter as this man did. How can he go on? How can one person handle so much grief? How did he cope with his wife and his other daughter's grief? How did he go to work each day? How could he ever smile again?

This same person also experienced the death of his cousin and her daughter in a freak accident not three months after the death of his daughter. Again, how does one person handle this level of tragedy in one lifetime?

The question becomes "How does this man keep going, having experienced the trauma of so many deaths?" Does he consider himself a religious person? No, he is not—not in the parochial sense of the word. His religious experience of loving others is his personality.

This man is the definition of quiet courage and a deep-seated faith in the concepts of love and compassion. This is a man without fear. He is not bitter, feeling that life has cheated him out of the time with his loved ones. He is not depressed; rather, he looks for something in each day to enjoy, whether it is something funny that his wife and daughter do, or something funny at work or just in life in general. He never lost his humor.

This quiet profile in spiritual courage is important to study because the overpowering trait that defines this man is his loving attitude. The love he feels inside of himself was never stunted, never shut down, never held back. In his view, how could he possibly love anyone in his life less? He never knows when a person's time will be done on Earth, so it is important to him to love each person with all of his heart as much as he can every day.

Does he still grieve for those amazing personalities who have graced his life? Of course he does—especially his daughter—and yet, he does not let his grief define him. He lets his life of quiet courage and profound love define him.

Everyone who knows him loves him. Everyone feels safe when they are with him, knowing that his tenderness with each person's feelings is something that lives within him. He has used all of these experiences with life and death to define his path and that path is being the same loving man he has always been, yet very much a wiser man, as well. He knows what it is like to chart a new course and to live a different life after each person he has loved has left the Earth plane.

Today's society gives press to the rich and famous, but they do not know that there is a man whose spiritual wealth is so vast that there is no end to his love, no way to define a love as great as this man has for all people. Is he a saint? He would tell you "Oh, no!" But you can look at this quietly courageous man and imagine that perhaps the saints of old could take a lesson from the love he displays with such a tremendous generosity and could know that goodness surely lives on Earth in the form of this wonderful man.

Finally, is he alone? No. There are many, many men and women (including his wife and oldest daughter) just like him, who never shut off their love for others, never stopped caring and giving. Without these people, the world would be a much darker place. All of them had a choice in how they would handle tragedy. They chose love; and in that choice, they also chose the path of wisdom and healing. How fortunate we are to have these people as wonderful examples for us all to follow as we evolve on our own spiritual paths and face the often, towering experiences that living and dying have to offer.

This profile is dedicated to my brother–in–law Craig Harris with my deepest and most profound respect.

Tina Erwin

Endnotes

[1] Grant, *The Place We Call Home*, 29.
[2] Ibid., 176–177.
[3] Ibid., 170.
[4] Ibid., 27.
[5] Ibid., 28–29.
[6] Ibid., 31.
[7] Ibid., 144–145.
[8] Ibid., 161.
[9] Ibid., 33.
[10] The Foundation for Inner Peace, *A Course in Miracles*, 3.
[11] Ibid.
[12] Ibid., 4–5.

Selected Bibliography

Albom, Mitch. *Tuesdays with Morrie*. New York, NY: Doubleday Publishing, 1997.

Alder, Vera Stanley. *The Finding of the Third Eye*. York Beach, Maine: Red Wheel/Weiser, 1970.

Alper, Frank. *Universal Law*. Phoenix, AZ: Arizona Metaphysical Society, 1986.

Altea, Rosemary. *Proud Spirit*. New York, NY: Eagle Brook, 1997.

Bailey, Alice A. *A Treatise on Cosmic Fire*. New York, NY: Lucis Press, Ltd., 1995.

Bailey, Alice A. *A Treatise on White Magic*. New York, NY: Lucis Press, Ltd., 1997.

Besant, Annie, F.T.S. *Death and After*. Adyar, Madras, India: Theosophical Publishing House, 1906.

Besant, Annie, F.T.S. *Karma*. Adyar, Madras, India: Theosophical Publishing House, 1972.

Besant, Annie, F.T.S. *Reincarnation*. New York, NY: Theosophical Publishing Society 1892.

Besant, Annie, F.T.S. *The Ancient Wisdom*. Adyar, Madras, India: Theosophical Publishing House, 1959.

Besant, Annie, F.T.S. *The Building of the Kosmos*. London, UK: Theosophical Publishing House, 1894.

Blavatsky, H.P. *The Secret Doctrine*. Wheaton, IL: Theosophical University Press, 1962.

Chaney, Earlyne C. and William L. Messick. *Kundalini and the Third Eye*. City of Commerce, CA: Stockton Trade Press, 1980.

Crane, Joseph. *Blessings, Gifts & Deeds: Building Your Celestial Mansion*. Emeryville, CA: West Coast Productions, 1996.

Dalai Lama and Howard C. Cutler, M.D. *The Art of Happiness*. New York, NY: Riverhead Trade, 1998.

Dass, Ram and Paul Gorman. *How Can I Help?* New York, NY: Harmony, 1995.

Eadie, Betty. *Embraced by the Light*. New York, NY: Gold Leaf Press, 1994.

Foundation for Inner Peace. *A Course in Miracles*. New York, NY: Viking, 1996.

Gerber, Richard, M.D. *Vibrational Medicine*. Santa Fe, NM: Inner Traditions Bear and Company, 1996.

Grant, Robert J. *The Place We Call Home*. Virginia Beach, VA: A.R.E. Press, 2000.

Greenwood, Dr. Michael and Dr. Peter Nunn. *Paradox & Healing*. Victoria, BC, Canada: Atrium Publishers Group, 1994.

Hauck, Rex. *Angels: The Mysterious Messenger*. New York, NY: Ballentine Books, 1994.

Hay, Louise. *You Can Heal Your Life*. Santa Monica, CA: Hay House Inc., 1986.

Hoffman, Enid. *Huna: A Beginner's Guide*. Atglen, PA: Whitford Press, 1981.

King, D.D., Th.D., George. *A Book of Sacred Prayers*. Hollywood, CA: The Aetherius Society, 1993.

Lawrence, Richard. *The Meditation Plan*. London, UK: Judy Paitkus Ltd., 1999.

Lawrence, Richard. *Unlock Your Psychic Powers*. London, UK: Souvenir Press, 1993.

Leadbeater, C.W. *The Devachanic Plane or the Heaven World*. Madras, India: Theosophical Publishing House, 1963.

Leadbeater, C.W. *The Hidden Side of Things*. Adyar, Madras and Benares, India: Theosophical Publishing House, 1913.

Levine, Stephen and Ondrea Levine. *Embracing the Beloved*. New York, NY: Doubleday, 1996.

Linn, Denise. *Past Lives, Present Dreams.* New York, NY: Ballentine Books, 1997.

Long, Max Freedom. *The Secret Science Behind Miracles.* Marina del Rey, CA: Devorss, 1976.

Long, Max Freedom. *The Secret Science Behind Work.* Marina del Rey, CA: Devorss, 1953.

Mark, Barbara and Trudy Griswold. *Angel Speake.* New York, NY: Simon and Schuster, 1995.

Mickaharic, Draja. *Spiritual Cleansing.* York Beach, Maine: Weiser Books, 1982.

Moolenburgh, H.C. *A Handbook of Angels.* Essex, UK: The C. W. Daniel Company Limited, 1993.

Myss, Caroline, Ph.D. *Anatomy of the Spirit.* New York, NY: Three Rivers Press, 1996.

Myss, Caroline, Ph.D. *Why People Don't Heal and How They Can.* New York, NY: Three Rivers Press, 1997.

Newhouse, Flower. *Here Are Your Answers.* Escondido, CA: Christward Ministry Publications, 1948.

Pohle, Nancy C. and Ellen L. Selover. *Awakening the Real You: Awareness Through Dreams and Intuition.* Virginia Beach, VA: A.R.E. Press, 1999.

Redfield, James. *The Tenth Insight.* New York, NY: Warner Books, 1996.

Rinpoche, Sogyal. *The Tibetan Book of Living and Dying.* San Francisco, CA: Harper Collins, 1994.

Roman, Sanaya. *Spiritual Growth.* Tiburon, CA: H.J. Kramer Inc., 1989.

Roman, Sanaya and Duane Packer. *Creating Money.* Tiburon, CA: HJ Kramer Inc., 1988.

Server. *The Science of the Initiates.* New York, NY: Lucis Publishing, 1934.

Subbarayudu, T.C., *The Doctrine of the Heart.* Adyar, Madras, India: Vasanta Press, 1947.

Urantia Foundation. *The Urantia Book.* Chicago, IL: Urantia Foundation, 1993.

Walsh, Neale Donald. *Conversations with God Book 1.* New York, NY: G.P. Putnam's Sons, 1996.

Walsh, Neale Donald. *Conversations with God Book 2.* Charlottesville, VA: Hampton Roads Publishing Company, Inc., 1997.

Walsh, Neale Donald. *Conversations with God Book 3.* Charlottesville, VA: Hampton Roads Publishing Company, Inc., 1998.

Weiss, Brian L. *Many Lives, Many Masters.* New York, NY: Fireside, Simon and Schuster Inc., 1988.

Zukav, Gary. *The Seat of the Soul.* New York, NY: Fireside, Simon and Schuster Inc., 1990.

EDGAR CAYCE'S A.R.E.

What Is A.R.E.?

The Association for Research and Enlightenment, Inc., (A.R.E.®) was founded in 1931 to research and make available information on psychic development, dreams, holistic health, meditation, and life after death. As an open–membership research organization, the A.R.E. continues to study and publish such information, to initiate research, and to promote conferences, distance learning, and regional events. Edgar Cayce, the most documented psychic of our time, was the moving force in the establishment of A.R.E.

Who Was Edgar Cayce?

Edgar Cayce (1877–1945) was born on a farm near Hopkinsville, Ky. He was an average individual in most respects. Yet, throughout his life, he manifested one of the most remarkable psychic talents of all time. As a young man, he found that he was able to enter into a self–induced trance state, which enabled him to place his mind in contact with an unlimited source of information. While asleep, he could answer questions or give accurate discourses on any topic. These discourses, more than 14,000 in number, were transcribed as he spoke and are called "readings."

Given the name and location of an individual anywhere in the world, he could correctly describe a person's condition and outline a regimen of treatment. The consistent accuracy of his diagnoses and the effectiveness of the treatments he prescribed made him a medical phenomenon, and he came to be called the "father of holistic medicine."

Eventually, the scope of Cayce's readings expanded to include such subjects as world religions, philosophy, psychology, parapsychology, dreams, history, the missing years of Jesus, ancient civilizations, soul growth, psychic development, prophecy, and reincarnation.

A.R.E. Membership

People from all walks of life have discovered meaningful and life–transforming insights through membership in A.R.E. To learn more about Edgar Cayce's A.R.E. and how membership in the A.R.E. can enhance your life, visit our Web site at EdgarCayce.org, or call us toll-free at 800–333–4499.

Edgar Cayce's A.R.E.
215 67th Street
Virginia Beach, VA 23451–2061

EDGARCAYCE.ORG